CRISIS INTERVENTION

Crisis Intervention
SECOND EDITION

WITHDRAWN

Edited by:
Lawrence Cohen, Ph.D.

University of Delaware
Newark, Delaware

William Claiborn, Ph.D.

Director, Department of Mental Health
Mental Retardation
and Substance Abuse
Alexandria, Virginia

Gerald A. Specter, Ph.D.

Mental Health Manpower Planning Program
District of Columbia

Volume IV
Community–Clinical Psychology Series
Series Editor: William L. Claiborn

 **HUMAN SCIENCES PRESS, INC.**
72 Fifth Avenue
NEW YORK, NY 10011

Library of Congress Cataloging in Publication Data

Crisis intervention.   (Community-clinical psychology series, ISSN 0916-6669 ; v. 4)
    Includes index.
    1. Crisis intervention (Psychiatry)   2. Community mental health services.   I. Cohen, Lawrence H.
II. Claiborn, William L.   III. Specter, Gerald A.
IV. Series. [DNLM: 1. Crisis intervention. WM 401 C9319]

RC480.6C734 1983	362.2'2	83-76
ISBN0-89885-107-6ISBN0-89885-108-4		(pbk.)
ISSN 0196-6669		0196-6669

CONTENTS

CONTRIBUTORS

Stephen M. Auerbach, Ph.D. is Associate Professor of Psychology at Virginia Commonwealth University

William L. Claiborn, Ph.D. is Director, Department of Mental Health, Mental Retardation and Substance Abuse, City of Alexandria, Virginia

Lawrence H. Cohen, Ph.D. is Assistant Professor and Director of the University of Delaware.

Rita Yopp Cohen, Ph.D. is a Research Psychologist in the Department of Psychiatry, University of Pennsylvania.

Clyde A. Crego, Ph.D. is Director of the University of Counseling Center at California State University, Long Beach.

Marilyn Wendland Crego, Ph.D. is now living in Southern California after several years serving as Assistant Dean of the Faculty at Stephens College in Columbia, Missouri, where she was also Director of the School of Liberal & Professional Studies.

Joseph A. Durlak, Ph.D. is Associate Professor in the Applied Psychology Program, Loyola University of Chicago.

Theodore Franklin, Ph.D. is a psychologist in private practice in Marina del Rey, California. He has served as a consultant with the Los Angeles Suicide Prevention Center and Institute for the Study of Destructive Behaviors and participated in the development of the NIMH Training Manual for Human Service Workers in Major Disasters.

John Kafat, Ph.D. is Director, Department of Training, St. Clare's Hospital CMHC and Contributing Faculty, Rutgers University Graduate School of Applied and Professional Psychology.

Dean G. Kilpatrick, Ph.D. is Professor, Department of Psychiatry and Behavioral Sciences, Medical University of South Carolina.

Michael W. Kirby, Ph.D. is Director of Research and Evaluation, Southwest Denver Community Mental Health Services, Inc.

Dean W. Nelson, M.A. is a graduate student in clinical psychology at the University of Delaware.

7

Paul R. Polak, M.D. was Executive Director, Southwest Denver Community Mental Health Services, Inc., and currently has a practice as a consulting psychiatrist.

Judith A. Roth, M.A. is the "Network" Trainer and Supervisor, Jackson County Community Mental Health Center, Carbondale, Illinois.

Karl A. Slaikeu, Ph.D. is Associate Professor of Psychology and Director of the Psychological Services Center at the University of South Carolina.

Gerald A. Specter, Ph.D. is Chief of the State Mental Health Manpower Planning Project for the District of Columbia.

Lois J. Veronen, Ph.D. is Assistant Professor of Psychology in the Department of Psychiatry and Behavioral Sciences at the Medical University of South Carolina.

Theodore C. Weerts is the Director of Adult Psychiatric Services, Southwest Denver Community Mental Health Services, Inc.

PREFACE

The original publication of *Crisis Intervention* in 1973 was the successful outgrowth of one of a continuing series of symposia at the University of Maryland on topical issues in community-clinical psychology. The meeting on crisis intervention, held in March of 1972, included mental health workers from around the country. Presenters and participants alike were active in theoretical, clinical, and evaluative aspects of crisis intervention services; they represented a variety of disciplines, orientations, and beliefs. The chapters in the original edition of this book included most of the formal presentations from that symposium.

Over the past decade, the scope of what is considered crisis intervention has broadened, so far as to include many things not formally thought of as crises. Should all aspects of life come to represent crises (such as a continuous series of developmental crises), then the uniqueness of both a crisis and crisis intervention disappears. Crisis theory then must compete directly with other theories of personality and behavior change. Scattered throughout this volume are several indications that crisis work has begun to include rather "ordinary" problems in living. Despite this, the challenges inherent in each of these new crises provide a focus on new, enthusiastic approaches to previously neglected mental health needs.

We commented in the original edition on the limited practical utility of crisis theory and urged readers to contribute to the refinement of the theoretical underpinnings of crisis intervention strategies. We can repeat that exhortation today. The nine intervening years seem not to have added much to theory, although crisis intervention programs have multiplied, many descriptive articles have been written, and some evaluative research has been reported. Crisis workers today seem content (or are forced) to continue their work with little more than formal reference to the seminal but limited theoretical contributions of Lindemann, Caplan, Shneidman, and

9

others. We speculated that the training of professionals, which emphasizes the lengthy dynamic method of personality change, might make it difficult for them to accept a crisis model of mental health intervention. It seems that events of intervening years show that concern to have been misplaced. Theoretical prescriptions in general seem to be playing less a part of mental health practice than in prior years.

Providers of services have to "make do" with their resources at hand and cannot default on care for someone in great need for lack of a cogent or verified theory. (A consequence, of course, is that many of the efforts of crisis workers may be counterproductive, inefficient, impotent, or worse, and there is no easy way to assess the value of an approach, to teach it to others, or to predict outcomes.) Despite these limitations in theory, the examples in this book convey a sense of action and excitement, and of professional responsibility for well-delivered, effective crisis services.

The original volume contained several discussions of the appropriate roles of the professional and paraprofessional in crisis work. Controversy over role definition continues today. We have included some current writing on the subject, but the reader will discern that this issue has not been fully resolved. Some of the difficulty can be resolved by understanding the context: a police officer is often necessarily the first social system worker on the scene in a crisis and could presumably need and use some "first mental aid" skills even if the next step was to call a mental health professional (although some writers would not include this first aid under the rubric of crisis intervention). Both the police officer and the mental health professional contribute to the crisis intervention—each with unique perspectives, opportunities, and limitations. Not withstanding the definitional and semantic aspects of the debate, there are real questions about what are the skills required for specific crisis intervention and who can and should be trained to possess these skills. This book gives several alternate approaches to the selection and training of crisis workers.

In preparing this revised volume, we decided to include entirely new material rather than republish some of the original and still valuable articles. The current sampling represents both a review of the basic definitions and concepts covered in the first edition and a different set of examples of application. Used together the two books give a fairly broad perspective on crisis work; this volume alone offers a sufficient view of the field as it currently exists.

As in most applied areas, crisis work is subject to fads. While time puts old fads in perspective, current fads are harder to detect. We suspect that we are not immune to short-sighted overvaluation of current "new" crisis service ideas. As the *zeitgeist* changes, so does our sense of what is important and unique. Rape crisis work, for example, has received special support from the Congress through NIMH (National Institute of Mental Health). The initiative can be seen to reflect a long needed awareness of the poor assistance given to rape victims in the past, but it also may represent a temporary change in the allocation of resources fostered by an externally created (federally funded) impetus to develop a community based response mechanism for this type of crisis. Whereas these rape crisis centers began as true indigenous responses to individual community needs, the same is less true for many of the funded programs. Once federal (or state) departments begin to support special services, the opportunity for innovation and uniqueness diminishes. Analogies can be drawn to so called "disaster crisis" programs and hot lines, drug programs, and others. The identification of passing trends, or short term distortions in the allocation of resources, should not be construed as a criticism of the individual projects or a devaluing of the real and unmet needs of those in crisis. For the longer view, a comparison of rhetoric between the two volumes in this regard is a useful exercise.

If you are someone who does crisis work, trains crisis workers, evaluates crisis programs, or theorizes about the crisis concept, there are a number of helpful chapters in this book. There are some good examples of training programs for indigenous workers and some sound conceptualization of crisis intervention strategies. Most of these examples can be viewed more generally than the limited context of the chapters might suggest. For example, the ideas about adult learners discussed in the chapter on police training by Crego and Crego are useful in any program that deals with adults. Readers should find themselves with a good sense of the field, capturing the excitement and enthusiasm of the authors, and with a good critical sense by which to judge the merits of the approaches endorsed by the contributing authors.

The original editors have been joined in this volume by Lawrence Cohen who has been responsible for most of the hard work of coordinating the authors and manuscripts in various states of review. We would like to express our appreciation to Norma Fox of Human Sciences Press for her encouragement of this project and to Barbara Parker who managed most of the final manuscript typing.

Newark, Del.; Washington, D.C.
LC, WC, GS

Chapter 1

CRISIS INTERVENTION: AN OVERVIEW OF THEORY AND TECHNIQUE

Lawrence H. Cohen
Dean W. Nelson

The purpose of this introductory chapter is to provide an overview of the theory and technique of crisis intervention, broadly conceived. This chapter presents: the major assumptions of crisis theory; a description of the common techniques employed by crisis interveners; an historical and conceptual perspective on crisis intervention as a form of mental health treatment; and some critical comments on the widely accepted, but virtually unresearched, assumptions of crisis theory and crisis intervention. It should be mentioned at the outset that we have not prepared an original theoretical piece on crisis intervention; much of the material presented in this chapter, especially the first three sections, represents a synthesis of ideas gleaned from an extensive review of the crisis literature.

THE ASSUMPTIONS OF CRISIS THEORY

Almost all of the current assumptions of crisis theory stem from Caplan's (1964) classic conceptualization of preventive psychiatry, which borrowed generously from ego-psychological principles.

13

According to Caplan, individuals in noncrisis states maintain a level of emotional homeostasis, in which stress is successfully handled by habitual problem-solving abilities. When a situation is such that these abilities represent inadequate coping resources, an individual may experience a crisis reaction. A crisis, therefore, is defined as an imbalance between the perceived difficulty and significance of a threatening situation and the coping resources available to an individual.

Caplan (1964) specified a developmental sequence characterizing a crisis reaction. In the first stage, a threatening situation elicits feelings of anxiety, which are followed by a reliance on habitual problem-solving strategies in efforts to restore emotional equilibrium. In the second stage, these problem-solving strategies fail to restore equilibrium, which further exacerbates the individual's feelings of tension. Here, functioning may become disorganized and trial and error attempts at coping may appear. The third stage is characterized by the generation of emergency and novel coping responses in an attempt to reduce anxiety. Such responses may include, for example, redefinition of the threatening situation or a modification of the individual's original goals. If these emergency measures fail, anxiety is further heightened, the individual reaches his or her *breaking point*, and personality disorganization follows. It is essential to understand that Caplan did not view a crisis reaction as a form of pathology, but instead a normal response sequence produced by a hazardous external event.

Caplan (1964) believed that a crisis represented a transitional period; it could lead to either some impairment in adjustment or growth in personality. For example, growth might occur due to the learning of a new coping response, and because the individual's self-concept is enhanced following a mastery experience. The variables that mediate an individual's adjustment to a crisis include the perception of the threatening event, the repertoire of coping responses, and the availability of social support. Thus, mediating variables include both psychological and environmental factors.

Caplan (1964) was equally emphatic in his assumption concerning the time-limited nature of crises. Crises last about 4 to 6 weeks, after which the individual experiences psychiatric impairment or growth. It is also assumed by Caplan that, during a crisis, an individual experiences an increased desire to be helped by others and is more open to interpersonal intervention than he or she would be during the state of emotional equilibrium.

The crisis literature (e.g., Aguilera & Messick, 1978) also distinguishes between situational and maturational crises. Situational crises, which are usually described as unanticipated external events, include, for example, death of a loved one, natural disasters, rape, or emergency medical hospitalization, and are seen as suddenly occurring hazardous events that often result in fairly stereotypic, or generic, reactions. The work of Lindemann (1944) is often cited as depicting the generic reaction to the death of a loved one, while the work of Burgess and Holmstrom (1974) is often cited as depicting the generic reaction to rape. The concept of a maturational (or developmental) crisis is more abstract and not totally consistent with the underlying assumptions of crisis theory. During such periods as adolescence or old age, an individual will be confronted with various developmental tasks that may be taxing on his or her coping resources, and the time frame of crisis reactions is extended to accommodate these types of experiences. It is assumed that certain situations or problems may emerge as crises during one developmental stage while they might not otherwise during another such stage (Golan, 1978). A maturational crisis may occur, therefore, because novel challenges are confronted (e.g., sexuality during adolescence) and/or because old coping strategies become problemmatical or ineffective (e.g., running to mother).

Caplan and others have elaborated on these basic assumptions of crisis theory. For example, Sifneos (1960) and Golan (1978) specify the following elements in a crisis: (a) the hazardous event, (b) the vulnerable state, (c) the precipitating factor, and (d) the state of crisis itself. Other writers (e.g., Aguilera & Messick, 1978) discuss the concept of a family crisis and the link between a current crisis and prior unresolved conflicts. Korner (1973) distinguishes between a shock and an exhaustion crisis; the former follows a sudden change in the environment, while the latter stems from a prolonged state of emergency. It is our impression, however, that Caplan's (1964) original conceptualization of crises has had an overriding influence on subsequent treatments of the topic.

CRISIS INTERVENTION TECHNIQUES

Similarly to short-term psychoanalytic psychotherapy and behavior therapy, crisis intervention is one form of brief intervention, although it does differ dramatically from the first two treatments on several dimensions. It is believed that crisis intervention, to be effective, must be readily available and need last no longer than 10 or 12 sessions. Clearly, crisis intervention should be provided immediately upon request; a delay of several days might fail to capitalize on the client's heightened emotional arousal and susceptibility to interpersonal intervention, and, more importantly, might fail to prevent psychiatric disturbance (Butcher & Koss, 1978).

Some writers (e.g., Jacobson, Strickler, & Morley, 1968) have classified crisis intervention into four types: (a) environmental manipulation, (b) general support, (c) generic crisis intervention, and (d) individually-tailored crisis intervention. In environmental manipulation, the intervener serves primarily as a referral source, linking the client with appropriate community and institutional resources. General support represents the provision of reassurance and interpersonal contact for a brief period of time. The generic approach involves the provision of services to individuals experiencing specific crises, and it presupposes a generic reaction to particular hazardous events; Caplan's approach would, for the most part, fall under this category. Individually-tailored crisis intervention is seen as a more in-depth form of treatment, in that it is assumed that the crisis is related in some way to the client's psychodynamic history. The following characteristics typify generic crisis intervention although there is considerable overlap among the various approaches.

Assessment is viewed as an integral component of crisis intervention, although it does differ from traditional diagnostic evaluation. Since crisis theory represents a departure from a medical, pathology oriented model, no attempt is usually made to *diagnose*, other than when such an assessment is essential to understanding the client's precrisis functioning or how a crisis is exacerbating a chronic psychiatric condition. Instead, assessment usually involves an understanding of the hazardous event, the client's coping repertoire and previous attempts at mastery, the client's environmental supports, and the client's current stage of crisis according to Caplan's developmental model. The crisis intervener is usually not interested in recording a detailed history; however, past development may be important in understanding the psychological meaning that the individual attaches to the current crisis. Assessment in crisis intervention may also include common psychiatric judgments of suicidal intent, homocidality, and mental status. In an interesting paper, Korner (1973) specified those aspects of the client that should be evaluated in a crisis assessment: (a) intellectual functioning, (b) interpersonal assets, (c) emotional resources, (d) level of hope, (e) motivation to help oneself, and (f) the extent to which the individual contributed to or worsened a threatening situation.

Butcher and Maudal (1976) provide an excellent description of common crisis intervention techniques. Their analysis reveals that crisis intervention often represents a hybrid approach combining the principles of behavior therapy and humanistic treatment. Crisis intervention, like behavior therapy, has as its primary goal the relief of symptoms. There is no attempt at reconstructive treatment; crisis intervention attempts to prevent further deterioration and restore the individual to a precrisis level of functioning. Given the brief nature of this treatment, it is usually recommended that the intervention be extremely focused and present oriented, and that discussion center on the precipitating event and the client's attempts (past and future) to cope with the threatening situation. Flexibility in scheduling is essential, as a once a week, 50 minute session is usually not the treatment of choice for an individual in crisis. The intervener often needs to depart from the traditional roles of a psychotherapist. Occasionally, the therapist must deal with the client's significant others, sometimes the entire family, and sometimes with other institutional service deliverers. The client is often encouraged to seek help and support from interpersonal and institutional resources in the community, and it is not uncommon for the intervener to serve as the client's advocate to other individuals and agencies.

As is true in all forms of treatment, the therapist must communicate to the client a sense of caring, optimism, and hope. Offering emotional support and empathic understanding is critical; the conveyance of an understanding of the client's feeling state will enhance the credibility of the therapist and assist in reducing the client's anxiety level. Providing factual information is often necessary, as misinformation and cognitive misperception may have contributed to the client's reaction. Because treatment is so brief, it is important that the therapist contract with the client to work on a narrowly focused set of concrete goals, and the therapist's communications must be concise and efficient. Once rapport has been established, the problem has been identified, feeling states have been explored, and the client's coping repertoire has been surveyed, an exploration of alternative coping responses is necessary. In general, unless the client is severely disorganized, advice and suggestions are kept to a minimum. Instead, most writers emphasize the colleagial nature of crisis intervention, with the therapist working with the client to generate potentially effective coping responses. Role playing might be appropriate, as might the prediction of future consequences of behavioral alternatives. Finally, a follow-up evaluation, if only by telephone, is important to determine if the client's precrisis level of functioning has been restored and if referrals have been successful.

AN HISTORICAL AND CONCEPTUAL ANALYSIS OF CRISIS INTERVENTION

A number of books and articles have outlined the historical developments that contributed to the theory and practice of crisis intervention (e.g., Aguilera & Messick, 1978; Butcher & Maudal, 1976; Caplan, 1964; Ewing, 1978). The major developments include: (a) treatment experiences during World War II, (b) the work of Eric Lindemann, (c) the writings of several ego analysts, and (d) the suicide prevention movement.

During World War II, it was discovered that the treatment of combat-related dysfunction (i.e., combat neurosis) was most effective if it was short-term in nature, provided immediately after detection, provided close to the front, focused on the immediate situational crisis, and encouraged the soldier to return to combat duty as quickly as possible. This treatment maintained the soldier in his unit and discouraged his adoption of a patient role. In Caplan's (1964) book, he cites a number of studies documenting the environmental influences on this combat reaction; the reaction was seen as related to the specific characteristics of the combat experience and the group cohesiveness of the soldier's unit, rather than the soldier's precrisis personality. Clearly, this treatment of combat neurosis incorporated the major principles of crisis intervention, although it was years before Caplan provided a conceptual model for such treatment.

In 1944, Lindemann published his classic article on grief reactions in the *American Journal of Psychiatry*. Based partly on his work with survivors of the Cocoanut Grove fire, this article describes the normal and morbid reactions to death of a loved one. Lindemann presented the acute grief reaction as a fairly stereotypic one, related more to the experience of loss than the premorbid personality of the griever. It is evident that Lindemann considered the grief reaction along the same lines that Caplan later conceptualized crises, which is not surprising given that the two men later collaborated at Harvard University. For Lindemann, the grief reaction was a specific stress disorder which was acute in onset and brief in duration, and which could be aided therapeutically in only 8 to 10 interviews. It should also be emphasized that Lindemann did not consider the grief reaction a type of mental disorder, but instead a time-limited struggle to cope with the experience of loss.

Aguilera and Messick (1978) and Golan (1978) discuss the contributions of the ego analytic theorists of the 1940s and 1950s to the development of crisis theory in the 1950s and 1960s. Such ego theorists as Hartmann and Rado modified traditional Freudian doctrine by discussing the importance of the present environment and the individual's attempts to adapt to the exigencies of current stress. Also, Erikson's writings of human development and the psychological crises characterizing the various developmental stages contributed to the conceptualization of maturational crises. One need only read Caplan (1964) to recognize the ego analytic flavor of much of crisis theory.

Finally, the suicide prevention movement of the 1950s and 1960s contributed greatly to the development of crisis theory and the provision of crisis intervention services. The British Samaritan Movement, established in the eary 1950s, and the Los Angeles Suicide Prevention Center, created in the late 1950s by Dublin, Farberow, and Shneidman, emphasized the immediate delivery of services, often by paraprofessionals, to individuals in crisis. The later development of telephone hot lines and drop-in centers, also manned primarily by paraprofessionals, can be traced to these early suicide prevention services.

Crisis Intervention as a Community Mental Health Service

Caplan (1964) believed that crisis intervention and consultation represented the core *clinical* services offered by a preventive psychiatrist. Conceptually, crisis intervention is quite compatible with a community mental health ideology, and the growth of crisis services parallels the development of the community mental health movement. In a number of textbooks on community psychology (e.g., Rappaport, 1977; Zax & Specter, 1974), there is a discussion of the various forces and factors that contributed to a community ideology in the 1960s, and it is instructive to note how the practice of crisis intervention emanated from very much the same forces. In this section, we will be selective in our discussion of the factors that contributed to a community ideology and the development of crisis-related services, singling out those that seem particularly relevant. Also, in recent years several writers (e.g., Goodstein & Sandler, 1978; Rappaport, 1977) have made the distinction between community mental health and community psychology, and while crisis intervention represents a community mental health service, it does not really constitute a community psychological activity.

First, the philosophy underlying the community mental health movement represents an application of public health principles to the field of mental health. Influenced by Lindemann, Caplan (1964) described the primary, secondary, and tertiary prevention efforts that could affect the mental health of a population. While crisis intervention can be conceptualized as either a primary or secondary prevention service, depending on the characteristics of the clientele, it is clear that this type of service is based on a public health model of mental health treatment.

Second, the controversy over the effectiveness of psychotherapy, which is still raging (Parloff, 1979), caused a number of practitioners to reconsider the necessity of long-term, intensive treatment, and contributed to a community mental health philosophy and the development of shorter-term, less traditional mental health services. Crisis intervention, which is seen as a brief, highly focused preventive strategy, represents an alternative to more lengthy, and often less cost efficient, services. As an aside, it is interesting to note that, to this date, the data seem to indicate that brief treatment, in general, is no less effective than longer-term treatment (Butcher & Koss, 1978).

A third factor that contributed to a community mental health ideology was the growing skepticism concerning the appropriateness of traditional psychotherapy for large numbers of individuals in need of service. Long-term, verbal, insight-oriented treatment might be appropriate for YAVIS (young, attractive, verbal, intelligent, and successful) clients (Schofield, 1964); however, large numbers of needy individuals possess nonYAVIS attributes. Crisis intervention, it would seem, is much less restrictive in terms of the characteristics of appropriate clients. With its goal of symptom relief, its brief time duration, and its present reality orientation, crisis intervention seems compatible with the needs and orientation of lower SES (socioeconomic status) individuals. Additionally, because an individual in crisis is supposedly highly receptive to interpersonal intervention, class and race barriers between the intervener and the client would seem to be less of an obstacle in crisis intervention than they might be in more traditional psychotherapy.

Fourth, the community mental health movement grew partly out of the concern that there was and would continue to be a shortage of mental health professional manpower. While there is some controversy over the appropriateness of paraprofessionals providing crisis services, most writers agree that, at least for generic crisis reactions, paraprofessionals can be effective service providers. Furthermore, it became apparent that crisis services, especially for generic reactions, could be effectively provided by natural care-givers in the community, such as the clergy, and that professionals could serve as consultants, teaching the principles of crisis intervention to other professionals and individuals who are more plentiful and accessible to individuals in crisis.

Finally, a fifth factor that led to the development of a community mental health ideology and that was consistent with the growth of crisis services was the growing dissatisfaction with the medical model of psychopathology. Theorists such as Szasz (1961) and Scheff (1966) criticized the medical model and popularized the concepts of *problems in living* and reactions to societal labelling (*secondary deviance*), respectively. Additionally, the behavioral theorists, especially psychologists, began to conceptualize most *mental disorders* not as illnesses, but as learned responses that were maladaptive (e.g., Ullmann & Krasner, 1969). As was mentioned previously, crisis theorists, such as Lindemann and Caplan, did not consider crises as pathological states, but merely as normal attempts to cope with threatening situations. Although crises may lead to forms of psychopathology if not adequately resolved within the time frame of several weeks, the immediate responses to crises were viewed as nonpathological reactions to stress.

A CRITIQUE OF CRISIS INTERVENTION

Although the theory of crisis intervention does have an intuitive appeal and is consistent with the popular model of community mental health, it is, we think, not unfair to point out that the assumptions of crisis theory remain highly speculative. For several decades, writers have articulated the assumptions of Lindemann and Caplan that crises last 4 to 6 weeks, that individuals in crisis are susceptible to interpersonal intervention, that crises are characterized by specific developmental stages, and that crises lead to either psychiatric disability or personality growth. As Auerbach points out in his chapter in this book, there are almost no data that either substantiate or refute these assumptions. In addition, more convincing data are required to document that there are indeed generic reactions to such hazardous events as rape and natural disasters (see Auerbach's, Franklin's, and Kilpatrick and Veronen's chapters in this book). It is possible that there are huge individual differences in reactions to hazardous events, the sequence characterizing these reactions, and the time frame encompassing this sequence, and, quite simply, it may be rather premature to advocate a general theory of crisis reactions. More sophisticated models of stress adaptation are currently being developed (e.g., Lazarus, 1974), and studies emanating from such models should help clarify the validity of many of the assumptions of crisis intervention.

Life Stress Research

It would seem that research on stressful life events holds great promise for clarifying the properties of crises and their relationship to psychopathology. Dohrenwend (1978), in fact, has developed a rudimentary flowchart that depicts the potential results of experiencing a hazardous event and the interventions that might prevent the development of psychiatric impairment. Although the relationship between the occurrence of stressful events and maladjustment may appear intuitively obvious, in fact, the empirical study of this relationship poses several complex conceptual and methodological problems. The first issue concerns the measurement of stressful life experiences. One could ask an individual if he or she experienced a number of events in the recent past, but when quantifying these experiences, does one rely on normative data on the *stressfulness* (i.e., the amount of readjustment required) of these events, or does one rely on impact ratings provided by the individual subject? A reliance on norm-based weightings of events requires a sensitivity to the representativeness of the normative group, because it appears that there are cultural differences in the readjustment required by certain hazardous events (Askenasy, Dohrenwend, & Dohrenwend, 1977). On the other hand, subjects' self-ratings of life experiences may be confounded with their status on personality variables, and any relationship between maladjustment and self-rated stressful experiences may be tautological in nature. From a theoretical perspective, it is important to understand the temporal relationship between stressful events and behavior, and regardless of the measurement strategy chosen, a prospective methodology would seem to be required, by which effects due to circumscribed life events can be partialled from those contributed by personality trait variables.

Additionally, more sophisticated measurement requires that life events be categorized on such dimensions as desirability/undesirability and independence/nonindependence. Previous research has suggested that desirable compared with undesirable life changes require less readjustment and are less strongly related to maladjustment (e.g., Sarason, Johnson, & Siegel, 1978; Vinokur & Selzer, 1975). Some hazardous events may occur independent of the individual's behavior/personality (e.g., death of a loved one, natural disasters, etc.), while the occurrence of other events may be linked to an individual's behavior or disposition (e.g., divorce, imprisonment, etc.). Moreover, some events, such as divorce, cannot easily be conceptualized as discrete experiences, in that they often produce sequelae of stressful experiences (e.g., child custody, reentry into the labor force, etc.) which potentially impact on functioning for an extended period of time.

More attention should be focused on variables that mediate individuals' reactions to specific types of threatening events. Variables such as locus of control, cognitive flexibility, sensation-seeking, physiological reactivity, availability of social support, etc. may influence the development of crisis reactions. Empirical study of the role of such moderator variables should enhance our understanding of the etiology of crisis reactions and result in the development of more targeted interventions.

Evaluation of Crisis Services

Despite the plethora of crisis-related services, the effectiveness of crisis intervention has yet to be adequately demonstrated. Clearly, outcome research in crisis intervention presents several methodological problems including: (a) the specification of the theoretical underpinnings of the intervention, (b) the specification of the intervention, (c) the determination of the critical intervention components, (d) the specification of the target population, (e) the operationalization of the intervention's proximal and distal objectives, and (f) attention to unanticipated and indirect outcomes. Although formidable, these problems are really not dissimilar from those inherent in the evaluation of any human service, and it is unfortunate that so little outcome data have been collected (Auerbach & Kilmann, 1977).

In conclusion, crisis intervention is a popular form of community mental health service and the chapters that follow document the variety of settings and clientele for which it is currently used. However, it is important to recognize that as a form of brief treatment based on a model of transitional disturbance, most assumptions about crisis intervention still remain unsubstantiated.

REFERENCES

Aguilera, D., & Messick, J. *Crisis intervention: Theory and methodology*. Saint Louis: Mosby, 1978.

Askenasy, A., Dohrenwend, B. P., & Dohrenwend, B. Some effects of social class and ethnic group membership on judgments of the magnitude of stressful life events: A research note. *Journal of Health and Social Behavior*, 1977, *18*, 432-439.

Auerbach, S.M., & Kilmann, P.R. Crisis Intervention: A review of outcome research. *Psychological Bulletin*, 1977, *84*, 1189–1217.

Burgess, A., & Holmstrom, L. *Rape: Victims of crisis*. Bowie, Md.: Brady, 1974.

Butcher, J., & Koss, M. Research on brief and crisis-oriented therapies. In S. Garfield & A. Bergin (Eds.), *Handbook of psychotherapy and behavior change*. New York: Wiley, 1978.

Butcher, J., & Maudal, G. Crisis intervention. In I. Weiner (Ed.), *Clinical methods in psychology*. New York: Wiley, 1976.

Caplan, G. *Principles of preventive psychiatry*. New York: Basic Books, 1964.

Dohrenwend, B. Social stress and community psychology. *American Journal of Community Psychology*, 1978, *6*, 1-14.

Ewing, C. *Crisis intervention as psychotherapy*. New York: Oxford University Press, 1978.

Golan, N. *Treatment in crisis situations*. New York: Free Press, 1978.

Goodstein, L., & Sandler, I. Using psychology to promote human welfare. *American Psychologist*, 1978, *33*, 882-892.

Jacobson, G., Strickler, M., & Morley, W. Generic and individual approaches to crisis intervention. *American Journal of Public Health*, 1968, *58*, 338-343.

Korner, I. Crisis reduction and the psychological consultant. In G. Specter & W. Claiborn (Eds.), *Crisis intervention*. New York: Behavioral Publications, 1973.

Lazarus, R. Psychological stress and coping in adaptation and illness. *International Journal of Psychiatry in Medicine*, 1974, *5*, 321–333.

Lindemann, E. Symptomatology and management of acute grief. *American Journal of Psychiatry*, 1944, *101*, 141-148.

Parloff, M. Can psychotherapy research guide the policy maker? A little knowledge may be a dangerous thing. *American Psychologist*, 1979, *34*, 296-306.

Rappaport, J. *Community psychology*. New York: Holt, Rinehart & Winston, 1977.

Sarason, I., Johnson, J., & Siegel, J. Assessing the impact of life changes: Development of the Life Experiences Survey. *Journal of Consulting and Clinical Psychology*, 1978, *46*, 932-946.

Scheff, T. *Being mentally ill: A sociological theory*. Chicago: Aldine, 1966.

Schofield, W. *Psychotherapy, the purchase of friendship*. Englewood Cliffs, N.J.: Prentice-Hall, 1964.

Sifneos, P. A concept of emotional crisis. *Mental Hygiene*, 1960, *44*, 169-170.

Szasz, T. *The myth of mental illness: Foundations of a theory of personal conduct*. New York: Hoeber-Harper, 1961.

Ullmann, L., & Krasner, L. *A psychological approach to abnormal behavior*. Englewood Cliffs, N.J.: Prentice-Hall, 1969.

Vinokur, A., & Selzer, M. Desirable versus undesirable life events: Their relationship to stress and mental distress. *Journal of Personality and Social Psychology*, 1975, *32*, 329-337.

Zax, M., & Specter, G. *Introduction to community psychology*, New York: Wiley, 1974.

Section I

PERSONNEL AND TRAINING IN CRISIS INTERVENTION

A primary question in crisis intervention is who should be performing the services. Only after it is decided who will be performing the crisis services can it be decided what training is required and how the training should occur.

In some cases, who the crisis worker should be is defined by the organization or institution supporting the interventions. For example, community mental health centers or hot lines can define by policy who shall offer the service under specified levels of supervision. However, when the service provider is not a mental health professional, working in a non-mental health context, there can be no further choice of provider. A police officer who faces a domestic crisis can not defer instantly to mental health professionals. Even if police are expected to call on backup professional mental health personnel as soon as possible, they would still need to provide "first aid" in the emotional crisis. In addition, the emotional aspects of many crises must be face by many human service workers (fire, social service, religious, educational, etc.) without the benefit of present mental health professionals. The debate over who is an appropriate crisis worker, therefore, can apply only to certain settings, or to certain roles (such as longer-term interventions), although the result of the debate can have major policy implications for the delivery of most human services.

Durlak and Roth, in Chapter 2, suggest that the requirements for staff, the prohibitive cost of using only professionals, and the research support for and the theoretical desirability of using "indigenous workers" are all factors contributing to both the reality and the desirability of using paraprofessional crisis workers. Their extensive discussion of the research on nonprofessionals suggests that there is little evidence that the professional is better at certain types of crisis work than the trained nonprofessional. Following their conclusion about the desirability of using paraprofessionals, Durlak and Roth discuss the methods of selection of workers: clinical assessment, self-selection, and behavioral prediction. They conclude that no method works exceptionally well. Finally, they discuss some of what they believe are key elements in the training of crisis workers, and include recommendations for the provision of strong administrative support to train and retain crisis workers.

Once it is determined who should do crisis work, it is necessary to decide what it is they should do and how to evaluate if they are doing it well. (Of course, some would suggest that deciding the "who" should occur only after the "what" is fully specified. As noted above, often the "who" is not an option, so the order of tasks presented here would apply.) How should crisis workers be trained? Can there be stable, valid standards of performance? Chapters 3 and 4 discuss some assumptions about training in greater detail. Kalafat, in Chapter 3, begins with the premise that training can be *competency* based. Kalafat's model involves specifying the skills, modeling the skills, practicing the new skills, giving feedback, and continuing practice. He believes that people in a crisis can be helped by proceeding through a 5-step generic helping strategy: (a) establishment of a relationship, (b) definition of the problem, (c) exploration of feelings, (d) exploration of past coping attempts, and (e) exploration of alternatives and development of an action plan.

The Cregos, in Chapter 4, outline a training-consultation model for use with police. They describe a training program for police workers who perform within their natural setting, and who have other, non-mental health, primary responsibilities and duties. In such circumstances, a consultative relationship between police management and the trainers during the planning and implementation phase is essential. The Cregos provide examples that illustrate the importance of understanding the motivations for and needs of participants in crisis training. A unique contribution of this chapter is an emphasis on the important characteristics of the adult learner, including analysis of how training can be tailored to match the special ways adults participate in an educational experience. The factors they mention include: level of motivation, cognitive abilities (and cognitive structure), ability to generalize, and limited willingness to take public risk.

The chapters in this section do not resolve the questions of who should be providing crisis services, what crisis services are, or even necessarily how workers should be trained to provide these services. However, it will become evident to the reader that professionals will not and cannot provide the full range of crisis services, so it is then necessary to consider who can contribute and how they should be trained and supervised. It becomes clear that "pat" formulas for training will not be effective and that a sophisticated approach to crisis intervention training will include an assessment of needs, a negotiated understanding between the trainer and trainee, focused skill development, and an attention to criteria of successful performance. The chapters in this section give a good overview of typical and exemplary training now occurring in the crisis intervention area.

Chapter 2

USE OF PARAPROFESSIONALS IN CRISIS INTERVENTION*

Joseph A. Durlak
Judith A. Roth

Most leaders in the field would agree that paraprofessionals have been instrumental to the growth, maintenance, and success of crisis intervention programs. The purposes of this chapter are to explain why generally positive sentiments exist regarding paraprofessionals and to discuss the major programmatic issues related to their effective use in crisis programs. Introductory comments define who parapro-fessionals are and indicate the services they usually perform. Next, the major reasons for using paraprofessionals as crisis staff are dis-cussed, and a summary of research data pertaining to their clinical effectiveness is presented. The remaining sections of this chapter describe the prominent issues involved in the selection, training, supervision, and administration of paraprofessional crisis staff. Wherever possible, an overview of current practices in the field is presented along with recommendations regarding the most effective or promising techniques related to optimal paraprofessional staff development.

*The authors wish to thank Chris Durlak and Therese May for their helpful comments on an earlier draft of this chapter.

33

Paraprofessionals are defined as those persons who have not received formal, postbaccalaureate training and education in professional mental health programs, and thus may possess an education ranging from grade school through college. The major groups of paraprofessionals include homemakers, students, parents, and senior citizens, as well as teachers, general physicians, and the clergy.

The settings and roles for paraprofessional crisis staff vary widely across at least four major dimensions. These include: (a) the method of service delivery (telephone, walk-in, or outreach work), (b) the type of service offered (information, referral, or counseling), (c) whether all problems are accepted or specific target problems are the focus of the service (such as rape, suicide, or drugs), and, (d) who receives the services (anyone in the community, or primarily certain groups such as college and university students, adolescents, runaways, families, rape victims, the bereaved, suicidal, or elderly).

The heterogeneity of roles and settings for paraprofessionals requires that the general commentary and recommendations offered here must be considered within the context of specific crisis programs. Therefore, the reader may find it useful to consult additonal references that provide specific guidelines (Delworth, Rudow, & Taub, 1972; McGee, 1974; Mills, 1977).

REASONS FOR USING PARAPROFESSIONALS IN CRISIS INTERVENTION

There are three major reasons for using paraprofessionals in crisis intervention. The first is essentially practical and relates to staffing considerations. The second is clinical and deals with paraprofessionals' abilities as helping agents, and the third involves theoretical arguments regarding the optimal delivery of human services.

Staffing Considerations

Recent data indicate that there are at least 200 suicide prevention/crisis intervention centers (McGee, 1974), over 1,000 telephone hot lines (National Exchange, 1973) and a minimum of 210 rape and women's crisis centers (Mills, 1977). Moreover, there are probably several hundred additional crisis-oriented programs operated by colleges and universities and community clinics. Allowing for some overlap in how these agencies are counted in different surveys, there are probably about 1,500 crisis-oriented programs in operation throughout the country.

McGee and Jennings (1973) estimate that between 10 and 90 persons are needed to staff a telephone crisis center depending on the nature of the center and length of each shift. Surveys of the staffing patterns of samples of rape and women's crisis centers (Mills, 1977) and general telephone hot lines (McCord & Packwood, 1973) suggest an average of about 40 workers per program.

Therefore, an estimated 60,000 personnel are needed to staff existing programs (range of from 15,000 to 135,000). There are simply not enough professionally trained workers to staff existing crisis services adequately. As a result, most programs could not operate without paraprofessionals willing to contribute their time and support.

It seems reasonable to estimate that 80-90% of current crisis staff are paraprofessionals. Based on average staffing patterns, this would mean there are between 48,000 and 54,000 paraprofessionals working in crisis programs each year, primarily as part-time volunteers.

Clinical Effectiveness of Paraprofessionals

Most programs use paraprofessionals not only because they are available personnel but also because it is believed paraprofessionals can be effective in helping roles. Fortunately, there is considerable evidence to support this belief.

The research literature on paraprofessionals is so extensive that only a brief overview can be presented here. By the end of 1979 there were over 1,700 published studies involving paraprofessional therapists, including 51 in the area of crisis intervention. Approximately 1,000 of these publications are outcome studies. The remainder are concerned with selection, training, and supervision, or are process investigations. Specific details on the published literature involving paraprofessionals can be found in three content-coded research bibliographies that are available for a nominal fee (Durlak, 1972; Durlak & Gillespie, 1978; Durlak & Heerboth, 1982).

Although many methodological issues remain unresolved, most paraprofessional outcome studies report positive results. Moreover, paraprofessionals have successfully participated in programs that span the entire range of client populations, treatment techniques, target problems, and clinical settings. In 42 direct comparisons, data indicate that the clinical outcomes paraprofessionals achieve are at least as good as, and, in some cases, significantly better than, those obtained by professionals (Durlak, 1979).

Studies examining paraprofessionals' functioning in crisis programs are also generally positive but there have been some disquieting findings. In his evaluative review, France (1975) concluded that trained paraprofessionals perform at levels that are at least minimally acceptable whereas untrained workers do not. For the most part, later studies have confirmed France's conclusion. However, conclusions regarding the abilities of paraprofessional crisis staff are limited to the communication skills paraprofessionals demonstrate over the telephone. Paraprofessional functioning in the other major roles they assume in crisis programs (such as referral agent or outreach worker) has not yet been adequately investigated.

The most provocative data in support of paraprofessionals' abilities come from a number of studies that have directly compared the clinical functioning of paraprofessional and professional staff. Getz, Fujita, and Allen (1975) asked 104 clients to evaluate the helpfulness of crisis services they received in the emergency room of a community hospital. There were no differences in the ratings provided by clients who were seen by paraprofessional or professional counselors. Similarly, DeVol (1976) reported no differences in client evaluations of services as a function of the level of paraprofessional or professional training and education of the counseling staff. One study compared paraprofessionals' and professionals' clinical judgments regarding the criteria for referring clients (Walfish, Tulkin, Tapp, & Russell, 1976). Findings suggested that the 10 professionals and 46 paraprofessionals were in general agreement about the most important criteria for inappropriate and appropriate referrals.

Two studies obtained independent ratings of workers' clinical performance during real or simulated crisis calls. O'Donnell and George (1977) trained 40 college students to portray five different crisis situations over the telephone and then evaluated four counseling groups when they responded to these called-in situations. The four groups consisted of 10 professional community mental health center staff, 10 experienced and trained paraprofessionals with a minimum of 1 year on-the-job experience at a telephone hot line, 10 recently trained but inexperienced paraprofessionals, and 10 college sophomores who had no interest in or involvement with telephone hot line work. Independent judges rated workers' global clinical performance and their functioning in seven specific areas such as empathy, concreteness, and problem-solving style. The two paraprofessional groups did not differ significantly from the professional group on any of the measures and all three groups consistently outperformed the college student controls.

In the final comparative study, Knickerbocker and McGee (1973) also compared paraprofessionals' and professionals' clinical performance when managing crisis situations. Taped segments of actual calls made to a crisis center and handled by 65 paraprofessional and 27 professional staff were evaluated along several clinical dimensions by independent raters. Paraprofessionals performed significantly better than professionals on a measure of therapeutic warmth. Results approached significance and also favored paraprofessionals on three other measures (empathy, a second measure of warmth, and a global assessment of therapeutic style). There were no significant between-group differences on the remaining four measures.

Two important qualifications must be made regarding the evaluation of paraprofessional crisis staff. First, much more work is needed to establish clear performance standards for crisis work and to relate these standards to desired client outcome. For example, we do not know what levels of clinical performance lead to what specific behavioral and affective changes in clients. In effect, conclusions regarding paraprofessionals' abilities must be offered in consideration of the current "state of the art" of research methodology in crisis intervention. Second, the number of research studies assessing paraprofessionals is meager relative to the extent to which these workers have been used in crisis programs. Both intrastudy and interstudy comparisons suggest considerable individual variability in performance (Durlak, 1979). Such findings suggest that whereas some paraprofessionally-staffed programs may be offering high quality services, others may not.

Nevertheless, various methods have been used to compare paraprofessionals' and professionals' crisis intervention skills. These include studying clinical judgments regarding the referral process, collecting consumer satisfaction ratings, and assessing worker performance during actual and simulated crisis calls. Regardless of the evaluation strategy, paraprofessionals have consistently performed as well as professionals.

Theoretical Arguments for Using Paraprofessionals

Community mental health and community psychology principles hold that the provision of helping services is a collective community effort, not the exclusive domain of professional personnel. Accordingly, professionals err by identifying crisis situations as mental health problems, and then insisting such problems require professionally trained personnel for their resolution. Sarason (1974) has noted that "... as long as the 'mental health problem' is defined in a way so as to require professional personnel for its solution, the situation is hopeless" (p. 88).

If the problem of inadequate professional resources for helping people in crisis is redefined as a community problem instead of a mental health problem, then it becomes the community's responsibility to rectify the problem. Thus, the professional can, if asked, share in the resolution of problems through consultation, supervision, and training, but is no longer exclusively responsible for providing crisis services. This would enable professionals to assist the community to marshall *its* own resources to meet *its* problems. Theoretically, this approach is considered far superior to the traditional approach of attempting to train more professionals, hoping that someday supply and demand will even out.

An added advantage in using paraprofessionals is the possibility of going beyond the resolution of crises to enhance the general quality of life in the community. For example, crisis staff may become sensitized to the need for social change after exposure to a variety of stressful conditions (e.g., family violence, unemployment, crime, etc.). As a result, citizen groups may be mobilized to implement needed community-based education, prevention, and social action programs. The payoff to the community comes from an increased sense of communal involvement and power, that is, "...the perception of similarity to others, an acknowledged interdependence with others, a willingess to maintain this interdependence by giving to or doing for others what one expects from them, and the feeling that one is part of a larger dependable and reliable structure'' (Sarason, 1974, p. 157).

Reasons for Not Using Paraprofessionals

McColsky (1973) has been the foremost critic of paraprofessional involvement in crisis services. She maintains that professional training is a necessary prerequisite for the management of psychological problems and that paraprofessional helping efforts, particularly in serious crisis situations, are crude, naive, and perhaps harmful. According to McColsky, the ideal crisis intervention model is one in which services are offered exclusively by professionals. In effect, McColsky's arguments rest upon the assumption that professionals are able to provide competent crisis intervention services whereas paraprofessionals are not. However, this assumption is not justified by current data.

For example, data from the comparative studies discussed previously indicate that at least some groups of paraprofessionals can function as adequately as professionals. Moreover, there are indications that the majority of professionals currently in training and those already in public service may not be adequately prepared (or motivated) to provide crisis services. Bloom and Parad (1977) surveyed the job activities of over 1,000 mental health professionals employed at 55 community mental health centers in 13 western states. These professionals devoted an average of less than 2 hours per week to crisis and emergency services. Furthermore, a significant portion of these professionals expressed a personal need for more training in crisis intervention.

In a recent survey, only 51% of 385 advanced doctoral students in clinical and community psychology indicated that the topic of crisis intervention was covered academically in their graduate curriculum (Zolik, Sirbu, & Hopkinson, 1976), and only 55% of these students were satisfied with their course coverage in crisis intervention. Similarly, although 2/3 of the 385 students reported that field experiences in crisis intervention were available in their training programs, only 37% of these students indicated that such experiences were adequate to satisfy their professional needs and interests.

In summary, one should not assume on a priori grounds that professionals are better prepared than paraprofessionals to function in crisis intervention programs or that there are any significant differences in the quality of services offered by these two helper groups. The critical variables appear to be effective training, supervision, and experience in crisis intervention. Whether or not individuals have attained the relevant clinical skills cannot be determined solely by examining their membership in so-called professional or paraprofessional groups.

The remaining sections of this chapter discuss several prominent issues in the selection, training, supervision, and administration of paraprofessional staff. It should be emphasized that the following program dimensions must be integrated for maximum staff performance. For example, it makes no sense to consider selection of paraprofessionals apart from their subsequent training. Likewise, the relative success of selection and training can be greatly affected by supervisory and administrative practices.

SELECTION

There are no standardized selection criteria for paraprofessional crisis workers. Nevertheless, it is possible to distinguish three strategies emphasized by different agencies.

Strategy 1: Clinical Assessment

Some programs assume that certain personality characteristics are necessary and that others are undesirable in crisis workers. The former may include emotional maturity, psychological-mindedness, interpersonal warmth, and ability to relate to people, while the latter are identified as the presence of psychological problems, rigidity, or insensitivity. Potential applicants are selected according to these clinical dimensions and the usual methods include individual or group interviews and psychological tests (McCord & Packwood, 1973).

Strategy 2: Self-selection and Training.

Other centers accept most applicants and depend on self-selection mechanisms plus subsequent training to produce a competent group of workers. The implicit assumption in this instance is that almost all individuals can learn to do crisis counseling effectively provided they are given adequate training and have the opportunity to become aware of what crisis counseling is and what the demands and expectations of their future roles will be. There is, in fact, some evidence supporting the assumption that training makes a relatively greater contribution than selection to the clinical performance of paraprofessionals (Ginsberg & Danish, 1979; Hart & King, 1979).

Strategy 3: Standardized Behavioral Procedures

Finally, some programs have developed standardized, behavioral methods to measure applicants' initial crisis intervention skills. To this end, questionnaires and/or behavioral assessments are used that sample the range of skills ultimately required on-the-job. The rationale for such selection procedures is based on Carkhuff's (1969) assertion that the best index of an individual's future clinical functioning is a measure of his or her current functioning. Although issues related to predictive validity have not yet been resolved, several promising behaviorally specific selection instruments and procedures have been introduced. (Gray, Nida, & Coonfield, 1976; Morgan & King, 1975; Tyler, Kalafat, Boroto, & Hartman, 1978).

At this time, Strategies 2 and 3 appear to be the most efficient and producive means of selecting paraprofessionals, and we recommend either of these procedures. We would discourage others from following the first strategy for numerous reasons. First, there is little if any evidence regarding what type of person is best suited for crisis work. Second, traditional diagnostic judgments of personality characteristics, particularly with respect to predicting future behavior, are of dubious validity. Third, the basis of subjective clinical judgments are seldom articulated in enough detail to replicate similar selection procedures in other settings. Finally, although there have been numerous research studies, personality and psychological tests have not yielded data that are of much practical use in the selection process.

As King, McGowen, Doonan, and Schweibert (1980) have recently emphasized, selection procedures must be implemented in consideration of the number of available applicants. Some programs have many more applicants than can be accepted, trained, and used, whereas others have only a small number of applicants. The former program can be selective even to the point of rejecting some potentially good workers. The latter program, however, cannot reject many potentially good workers even if it means taking some personnel who will eventually have to be released. In between these two extremes is the program with a moderate number of interested volunteers. This program must carefully balance selection decisions between accepting too many false positives and rejecting too many false negatives. Research that determines the most efficient decision-making process in each situation would make a significant contribution to the selection of paraprofessional staff.

TRAINING

Preservice training, inservice (on-the-job) training, and supervision are all closely related (or should be) in developing paraprofessionals' crisis-oriented skills. In discussing preservice training, we distinguish between the content of a training program and the techniques used to impart this content.

Contents of Preservice Training

Although any training can be extended or emphasized after paraprofessionals begin working, most workers will need preservice training in five major areas: (a) counseling techniques and intervention skills, (b) community resources, (c) ethics, (d) crisis theory, and (e) administrative and personnel issues.

Counseling skills in at least three major areas are important: (a) interpersonal communication and interviewing, (b) assessment, and (c) general and specific crisis intervention strategies. It is important that the crisis worker establish rapport and communicate understanding of and sensitivity to the client's situation. Thus, training in communication skills and/or instruction in active listening provides a basic clinical foundation for crisis work.

A natural tendency to give advice and react judgmentally can be curbed in most paraprofessionals by teaching them reflective listening skills and emphasizing the creation of a caring, positive relationship between crisis worker and client. In addition, paraprofessionals must be aware of their function as a role model for clients. In order to facilitate factual, present-oriented, and specific communications from a client, crisis workers can incorporate these characteristics into their own counseling style. Control is another important issue in training paraprofessionals. When the counselor establishes that he or she is in charge, anxiety is reduced and rapport is facilitated (Puryear, 1979). Conceptually, this issue may be foreign to many paraprofessionals and it is necessary to operationalize and demonstrate how counselors demonstrate control, for example, by limiting rambling and storytelling, and maintaining a problem solving focus. It is also important for the paraprofessional to be able to judge how much and when control should be exercised, to be comfortable when taking charge in certain situations, and when and how to begin giving control back to the client.

Paraprofessionals must also develop some facility in defining, assessing, and conceptualizing crisis situations. The maintenance of rapport while gathering information is, of course, crucial. Most trainees will need extensive practice in acquiring information through active listening and the use of open-ended questions. Providing trainees with a list of general questions which need to be answered during the assessment phase facilitates accuracy in defining the components of the crisis.

Two parts of the assessment process need special emphasis with paraprofessionals. The first is identifying who is in crisis. It is especially hard in the heat of a crisis to keep in mind that the identified client is perhaps not in crisis at all, whereas the person(s) labeling "the crisis" may in actuality be the client(s). For example, when the police bring in a person who "needs help," it is easy for counselors to accept the situation as given. However, this assumption may be invalid. The police might be experiencing a breakdown in problem solving and thus constitute "the crisis" in the sense of being the primary target of any intervention. Thus, it is important to emphasize with paraprofessionals the usefulness of independently assessing the situation as opposed to automatically accepting the view of involved parties.

Finally, trainees should be proficient in both general and specific intervention strategies. General strategies include such processes as formulating clinical goals, doing anticipatory planning, and making referrals. Trainees must be facile in defining workable problems and distinguishing between short- and long-term treatment goals. Paraprofessionals can easily become too idealistic in setting clinical goals and thus need to learn the value of conceptualizing and achieving short-term goals. Moreover, trainees will need practice in devising intervention plans that are specific and behaviorally focused. The more specific the plan, the more effective anticipatory planning will be. (Anticipatory planning involves the counselor helping the client to anticipate potential obstacles to carrying out a plan and to conceive of alternatives in advance.)

Specific crisis intervention strategies include the special skills relevant to the type of crisis the client is experiencing. Although it is not possible to train volunteers to work with every type of client, it is useful to include some preservice training relevant to the populations most frequently encountered at the center. For example, if the center is called upon frequently for help with drug crises, it would be useful for counselors to know how to: (a) check vital signs and determine whether a medical emergency exists, (b) use a *Physician's Desk Reference*, (c) be familiar with what information Poison Control will request during a consultation, (d) interpret drug slang, and (e) have a working knowledge of symptoms associated with various types of drug overdoses. For outreach teams, a knowledge of cardiopulmonary resuscitation is vital. Furthermore, different types of overdoses require different types of interventions. Other special populations that require special skills include sexual assault victims, suicidal clients, battered women, alcoholics, psychotics, and families in crisis. And of course, every center can benefit from ongoing training in dealing with that special population indigenous to all crisis centers: the chronic and/or manipulative client.

Crisis staff must know the local community's formal and informal *resources*. For example, paraprofessionals must acquire a working knowledge of what is available in the community in order to make appropriate referrals, involve community-based natural helping networks, and initiate environmental interventions. It is helpful if trainees visit local agencies and talk to their staff; interpersonal contact should enhance cooperation between agencies and improve referral making on the part of trainees.

Ethics constitute the third major content area to cover when training paraprofessional crisis workers. Perhaps the most salient ethical issue is that of confidentiality. Confidentiality may be easily compromised when many workers deal with the same client and when the atmosphere is more casual and there appears to be less distance between workers and clients. Therefore, it is of utmost importance that confidentiality be stressed repeatedly, perhaps as an ongoing part of inservice training and supervision.

Another issue that has ethical implications is the possible manipulation of clients. For example, a female alcoholic who needs a place to stay may be manipulated into checking into a detoxification facility as opposed to trying to find immediate shelter for herself. Is this ethical? Such issues do not have clear-cut guidelines and merit discussion in a group setting. As a corollary to these discussions, values clarification exercises are very helpful. Most paraprofessionals may be unaware of what values they hold on such issues as suicide and civil commitment and how their values may affect their crisis work; values clarification can offer a forum for discussion of such issues.

The fourth content area in training involves *crisis theory*. Trainees learn theory best when it is integrated with clinical practice. Such integration provides trainees with opportunities to anchor didactic learning to real life events. Nevertheless, trainees need preservice training in crisis theory to provide them with: (a) guidelines around which to orient their interventions, and (b) a basis for self-assessment of job performance.

Training should also include an explanation of *center policy* and *structure*. It is useful to develop a procedures manual that describes these areas in detail. The manual should include clear and specific information on: (a) job descriptions for each staff that include explanations of skills needed and clinical and administrative responsibilities and limitations, (b) opportunities and policies regarding upward mobility, (c) record-keeping requirements, (d) grievance procedures, (e) relevant local, state, and federal laws, (f) supervision and evaluation procedures, and (g) training requirements. In addition, details on the purpose, methods, and results of all program evaluations and research projects should be distributed to the staff as soon as reports are available.

To date, the most successful model for training paraprofessionals in clinical skills is one that relies on social learning principles (Durlak, 1982). Although different training programs attempt to teach different types of skills, trainers following a social learning orientation agree on the basic properties of effective training procedures. These include: (a) operational definitions of each clinical skill needed for the assigned helping role, (b) a pretraining assessment of trainees' competence in each skill, (c) an approach in which each clinical skill is taught and learned to criterion in a step-by-step fashion, (d) brief didactic instruction of how each skill is performed, (e) modeling of skills by competent practitioners, (f) opportunities for trainees to practice modelled skills under the trainer's supervision, (g) immediate performance feedback to trainees emphasizing positive reinforcement, (h) repetition of steps *d-g* until trainees achieve criterion mastery of each skill, and (i) a systematic posttraining assessment of trainees' skills.

There are several examples of programs that have successfully trained paraprofessionals in crisis intervention using social learning principles (Evans, Uhlemann, & Hearn, 1978; Sakowitz & Hirschman, 1975; Schinke, Smith, Myers, & Altman, 1979). We recommend that prospective trainers adopt a social learning emphasis to train crisis staff. Of course, the success of such an approach is dependent on specifying the roles paraprofessionals will be asked to perform and then operationalizing the skills and competencies needed to fulfill such roles. However, if these important preliminaries to training can be accomplished satisfactorily, then paraprofessionals can be taught a variety of specific skills and tasks in an effective and efficient manner.

SUPERVISION AND INSERVICE TRAINING

Many crisis programs underestimate the contribution of supervision and inservice training to paraprofessional staff development. Given the limited time that is usually available for preservice training, there is generally a need for inservice training in at least three main areas: (a) effective integration of crisis theory with clinical practice, (b) further training in working with special populations, and (c) additional clarification of values and ethics to insure that offered services are in clients' best interest. Furthermore, workers will need supervisory assistance as they attempt to apply the techniques they acquired in preservice training.

Several agencies have experimented successfully with peer supervision provided by advanced paraprofessionals as an adjunct to professionally-administered supervision. The use of peer supervision not only increases the likelihood that workers will receive prompt feedback regarding their job performance, but also is a means to recognize the work of competent volunteers by providing them with increased program responsibilities.

ADMINISTRATIVE ISSUES:
PROBLEMS AND POTENTIAL SOLUTIONS

Several major problems may develop when using paraprofessionals. We describe these problems first and then discuss strategies to solve them or prevent them from occurring.

Major Problems

McGee (1974) noted that morale problems, which may have multiple causes, are endemic in paraprofessionally-staffed programs. Paraprofessionals are apt to have continuous reservations and self-doubts about the adequacy of their performance and their impact on clients, as well as ill feelings regarding their working relationship with program administrators and supervisors (who are usually professionals). Relationship problems may stem from the paraprofessionals feeling overworked (or alternately underworked and undervalued) and/or shut out from meaningful participation in decision-making.

Attrition is another perennial problem. A high turnover rate may stem from morale problems within the agency or reflect more specifically on the failure of selection, training, and supervisory practices in developing competent and committed staff. At any rate, a high attrition rate represents a significant cost to the agency which is presented with a continual need to replenish its personnel.

Occasionally, administrators question if the use of paraprofessionals results in a definite pay-off to the agency when cost/benefit analyses are conducted. In most situations, two important benefits are derived from using paraprofessionals and usually outweigh attendant costs. First, the extensive use of unpaid volunteers represents a tremendous monetary savings compared to the finances needed to maintain a salaried staff. The second typical benefit is difficult to measure in monetary terms. As noted earlier, according to community mental health ideology, the use of paraprofessional change agents represents the optimal strategy for service delivery.

Despite significant benefits, many indirect costs accumulate in paraprofessional programs. There are the costs of professional staff time devoted to selection, training, supervision, and administration. These costs are increased when staff attrition rates are unacceptably high. Finally, there may be personal and emotional costs resulting from working in a program plagued by morale problems and interpersonal conflicts.

Possible Solutions

There are no guaranteed solutions to problems that arise in paraprofessional programs, but neither are any problems unsolvable. Our view is that the behavior and attitudes of the professional rather than the paraprofessional staff contribute more to the generation of the above administrative and personnel problems. Such a bold statement requires some elaboration.

Professionals typically function in a position of leadership and authority vis-a-vis paraprofessional staff. Initially, professionals are responsible for program goals, the method of service delivery, and establishing most of the parameters of the job setting. Therefore, paraprofessionals are highly dependent upon professionals for administrative, emotional, and technical support.

However, to make judicious use of paraprofessionals, professionals must truly be committed to the value of paraprofessional workers and willing to communicate trust and confidence in paraprofessionals' abilities. Moreover, professionals must be open to para-professionals' program input and permit paraprofessionals to exercise meaningful decision-making influence on agency procedures and goals. Finally, professionals must be oriented toward rewarding para-professionals for jobs well done. Rewards can be offered on an individual and group level through supervision and team meetings, on a formal level through systematic job evaluations, and on an administrative level through increased status and responsibility following effective on-the-job performance.

The latter issue is particularly important. Several programs have found it helpful to maintain multiple levels of paraprofessional staff. Essentially, numerous job categories are created to reward the most motivated and competent staff. Titles, activities, and the number of levels vary considerably. As an illustration, at Level 1 there may be front-line crisis staff (volunteers) who take regular weekly shifts answering the telephone or doing outreach work. At Level 2 there are specially selected workers (assistants) who supervise the volunteers or administer some other aspects of routine program services. At the third level are more specially chosen workers (associates) who super-vise the assistants and work closely with senior paraprofessional and professional staff in coordinating and organizing agency procedures and services. Various jobs and responsibilities can also be attained by workers within each level (e.g., fund-raising, training, etc.).

The most important elements of a diversified staffing structure are: (a) opportunities for both vertical and horizontal job mobility, (b) specific definitions of roles, responsibilities, and limitations of each job, and (c) detailed criteria for promotion into different job cat-egories including periodic review of workers' progress toward these criteria.

As a result of this hierarchical job structure, it should be ulti-mately possible for some paraprofessionals to hold at least equal power with professionals regarding program goals and practices. Experience suggests that in those situations where program directors recognize and reward staff members' personal commitment and leadership abilities, the likelihood of low morale, high attrition rates, or serious interpersonal conflicts among workers is greatly dimin-ished. Thus, administrative practices are important in enhancing agency functioning and reducing emotional and personal "costs" that may develop from unsatisfactory working conditions.

Rewarding the most competent paraprofessional staff with increased program responsibilities and status not only increases worker self-satisfaction and morale but is also a definite payoff by reducing program costs. That is, some skilled paraprofessionals can assume responsibilities for portions of the selection, training, and supervisory process, freeing professionals from having to perform these activities.

In general, the costs involved in selecting, training, and supervising paraprofessionals need not be high. The recommendations regarding these program practices were made with concern for maximum efficiency and productivity. For example, social learning training programs are relatively brief and can be adapted to suit multiple program goals. Moreover, selection and supervisory procedures that are closely integrated with training objectives also save considerable time, and may preclude a variety of personnel problems from surfacing by providing workers with clear expectations and feedback about their performance.

IMPORTANCE OF COMPETENT PROFESSIONAL STAFF

This chapter concludes by emphasizing that professionals must be adequately prepared for their roles in paraprofessionally-staffed crisis programs. For example, the literature clearly indicates that if paraprofessionals receive adequate training and supervision they can be effective helpers (Durlak, 1979). Therefore, it is incumbent upon professionals to provide these major program dimensions effectively. Unfortunately, survey data previously discussed (Bloom & Parad, 1977; Zolik, Sirbu, & Hopkinson, 1976) indicate that most professionals are probably not adequately trained in crisis intervention skills. The same surveys also indicate that most professionals are not experienced or skilled in working with paraprofessionals as trainers and supervisors. As a result, professionals often have to be selected much more carefully than paraprofessionals. McGee (1974) has emphasized that professionals may require the same training as offered to paraprofessionals. Most professionals will also need specific skill training in how to train and supervise paraprofessionals effectively (Durlak, 1982).

SUMMARY

Overall, the contribution that paraprofessionals have made to the field of crisis intervention is very positive. On a practical level, most programs could not be established and maintained without numerous paraprofessional volunteer staff. Furthermore, the influx of paraprofessionals into crisis programs is consonant with the community mental health and community psychology principle that the active participation of community residents is critical in the eventual resolution of local problems and the promotion of local resources. Finally, clinical data suggest that paraprofessionals are able to function effectively in crisis programs.

Several qualifications must be made when evaluating paraprofessional crisis workers. Current crisis intervention research is far from definitive and more assessment is needed to determine what skills are necessary for effective service delivery and what are the ultimate impacts of different forms of intervention. Moreover, many more paraprofessionally-staffed programs have been implemented than evaluated, suggesting that we do not know to what extent current positive findings regarding paraprofessionals' abilities are representative of the field as a whole. Finally, it is likely that issues relative to selection, training, supervision, and administration are as important, if not more important, factors affecting paraprofessionals' performance than any initial skills workers bring to the job.

Several recommendations regarding these program dimensions were offered in this chapter. For example, the most successful training techniques are those that follow social learning principles in targeting, developing, and maintaining desired job skills. Administratively, the programs that seem most successful are those that reward paraprofessionals' on-the-job performance with increased status and administrative responsibilities.

The use of paraprofessionals does mean a significant investment of time and energy on the part of professionals as well as favorable attitudes toward paraprofessionals' abilities and contributions. In addition, professionals need effective training and supervisory skills when working with paraprofessionals. Admittedly, many professionals may not have the personal and professional disposition and the clinical skills that are required to work most productively with paraprofessionals. Nevertheless, several groups of professionals and paraprofessionals have been able to integrate their complementary skills and resources to develop needed and seemingly successful crisis-oriented services. There is every reason to believe that these early successes in the field can, in large part, continue.

REFERENCES

Bloom, B. L., & Parad, H. J. Professional activities and training needs of community mental health center staff. In I. Iscoe, B. L. Bloom, & C. D. Spielberger (Eds.), *Community psychology in transition: Proceedings of the National Conference on Training in Community Psychology*. Washington, D.C.: Hemisphere Publishing Corporation, 1977.

Carkhuff, R. R. *Helping and human relations: Vol. 1: Selection and training*. New York: Holt, 1969.

Delworth, U., Rudow, E. H., & Taub, J. (Eds.). *Crisis center/hot line: A guidebook to beginning and operating*. Springfield, Ill: Charles C. Thomas, 1972.

DeVol, T. I. Does level of professional training make a difference in crisis intervention counseling? *Journal of Community Health*, 1976, *2*, 31-35.

Doyle, W. W. Jr., Foreman, M. E., & Wales, E. Effects of supervision in the training of nonprofessional crisis-intervention counselors. *Journal of Counseling Psychology*, 1977, *24*, 72-78.

Durlak, J. A. A content-coded research bibliography on the nonprofessional mental health worker. *JSAS Catalog of Selected Documents in Psychology*, 1972, *2*, 76-77. (Ms. No. 171).

Durlak, J.A. Comparative effectiveness of paraprofessional and professional helpers. *Psychological Bulletin*, 1979, *86*, 80-92.

Durlak, J.A. Training programs for paraprofessionals: Issues and guidelines. In A.M. Jeger & R.S. Slotnick (Eds.), *Community mental health: A behavioral-ecology perspective*. New York: Plenum, 1982.

Durlak, J. A., & Gillespie, J. F. Content-coded research bibliography on the nonprofessional mental health worker: 1972-1976. *JSAS Catalog of Selected Documents in Psychology*, 1978, *8*, 17-18 (Ms. No. 1652).

Durlak, J. A., & Heerboth, J. R. Content-coded research bibliography on the nonprofessional mental health worker: 1977-1979. *JSAS Catalog of Selected Documents in Psychology*, 1982, *2*, 23 (Ms. No. 2453).

Evans, D. R., Uhlemann, M. R., & Hearn, M. T. Microcounseling and sensitivity training with hot line workers. *Journal of Counseling Psychology*, 1978, *6*, 139-146.

France, K. Evaluation of lay volunteer crisis telephone workers. *American Journal of Community Psychology*, 1975, *3*, 197-220.

Getz, W. L., Fujita, B. N., & Allen, D. The use of paraprofessionals in crisis intervention: Evaluation of an innovative program. *American Journal of Community Psychology*, 1975, *3*, 135-144.

Ginsberg, M. R., & Danish, S. J. The effects of self-selection on trainees' verbal helping skills performance. *American Journal of Community Psychology*, 1979, *7*, 577-581.

Gray, B., Nida, R. A., & Coonfield, T. J. Empathic listening test: An instrument for the selection and training of telephone crisis workers. *Journal of Community Psychology*, 1976, *4*, 199-205.

Hart, L. E., & King, G. D. Selection versus training in the development of paraprofessionals. *Journal of Counseling Psychology*, 1979, *26*, 235-241.

King, G. D., McGowen, R., Doonan, R., & Schweibert, D. The selection of paraprofessional telephone counselors using the California Psychological Inventory. *American Journal of Community Psychology*, 1980, *8*, 495-501.

Knickerbocker, D. A., & McGee, R. K. Clinical effectiveness of nonprofessional and professional telephone workers in a crisis intervention center. In D. Lester & G. W. Brockopp (Eds.), *Crisis intervention and counseling by telephone*. Springfield, Ill: Charles C. Thomas, 1973.

McColskey, A. S. Models of crisis intervention: The crisis counseling model. In G. A. Specter & W. L. Claiborn (Eds.), *Crisis intervention*. New York: Behavioral Publications, 1973.

McCord, J. B., & Packwood, W. T. Crisis centers and hotlines: A survey. *Personnel and Guidance Journal*, 1973, *51*, 723-728.

McGee, R. K. *Crisis intervention in the community*. Baltimore: University Park Press, 1974.

McGee, R. K., & Jennings, B. Ascending to "lower" levels: The case for nonprofessional crisis workers. In D. Lester & G. W. Brockopp (Eds.), *Crisis intervention and counseling by telephone.* Springfield, Ill.: Charles C. Thomas, 1973.

Mills P. (Ed.) *Rape intervention resource manual.* Springfield, Ill.: Charles C. Thomas, 1977.

Morgan, J. P., & King, G. D. The selection and evaluation of the volunteer paraprofessional telephone counselor. *American Journal of Community Psychology,* 1975, *4,* 199-205.

O'Donnell, J. M., & George, K. The use of volunteers in a community mental health center emergency and reception service: A comparative study of professional and lay telephone counseling. *Community Mental Health Journal,* 1977, *13,* 3-12.

Puryear, D. A. *Helping people in crisis.* San Francisco: Jossey-Bass, 1979.

Sakowitz, M. L., & Hirschman, R. Self-ideal congruency and therapeutic skill development in nonpaid paraprofessionals. *Journal of Community Psychology,* 1975, *3,* 275-280.

Sarason, S. B. *The psychological sense of community: Prospects for a community psychology.* San Francisco: Jossey-Bass, 1974.

Schinke, S. P., Smith, T. E., Myers, R. K., & Altman, D. C. Crisis-intervention training with paraprofessionals. *Journal of Community Psychology,* 1979, *7,* 343-346.

The National Exchange. *Director of hot lines, switchboards, and related services.* Minneapolis, Minn: Author, 1973.

Tyler, M., Kalafat, J. D., Boroto, D. R., & Hartman, J. A brief assessment technique for paraprofessional helpers. *Journal of Community Psychology,* 1978, *6,* 53-59.

Walfish, S., Tulkin, S. R., Tapp, J. T., & Russell, M. Criteria for appropriate and inappropriate referrals to a crisis clinic. *Community Mental Health Journal,* 1976, *12,* 89-94.

Zolik, E., Sirbu, W., & Hopkinson, D. Perspective of clinical students on training in community mental health and community psychology. *American Journal of Community Psychology,* 1976, *4,* 339-349.

Chapter 3

TRAINING FOR CRISIS INTERVENTION

John Kalafat

This chapter will provide an overview of a competency-based training program in crisis intervention. The detailed training program is described in a complete manual and will only be highlighted here (Kalafat, Note 1). The emphasis will be on the origin and rationale for both the content and methodology of the training program. A strategy for developing training approaches and specific training techniques will be described.

Competency-based training is developed by identifying specific core behaviors, knowledge bases, and attitudes that characterize effective performance of a job, and training individuals in these skills, concepts, and attitudes (i.e., competencies) until they are clearly performing at an acceptable level (Klemp, 1980). The necessary competencies are identified through a task analysis which consists of specifying the nature of the job and identifying the specific demands involved in carrying out the job. Competencies are also identified by observing what can be agreed upon as superior performers and specifying what they do and do not do as compared to less effective performers (Klemp & Spencer, 1980).

It must be emphasized that what has been described is a continual feedback process. That is, in vivo job demands and worker performances are constantly monitored as the sources for relevant training contents and strategies. The training process and content are in turn continuously checked against the in vivo task in order to ensure that trainees are acquiring the necessary job-relevant competencies.

The application of this approach to training crisis workers has led to specific training strategies and contents. The training program to be described was developed in a community crisis service that provided telephone crisis intervention as well as mobile outreach teams to an eight-county region.

JOB ANALYSIS

A crisis, by definition, is a stressful situation in which a demand is placed on an individual for a response that is not in his or her repertoire, or is in the repertoire but is currently unavailable due to fatigue, anxiety, or some other mitigating circumstance. There are a number of features of the crisis situation that place unique demands on the intervening individual or agency.

This definition emphasizes a nonpathological, ecological view of crises. A crisis results from a particular combination of an individual with a coping repertoire that contains both strengths and weaknesses and a situation that contains both stressful and supportive elements. This definition implies that *everyone* can and does experience crises which can be of a very wide variety in nature. What this means for crisis intervention is that there is no selection as to type of client or problem as a basis for service eligibility, that interventions can be aimed at individuals, environments, or both, and that clients, while they may be dysfunctional to varying degrees, should not be treated as pathological or incompetent.

Crises are also understood to be critical turning points in which individuals are more open to change and will either adopt effective coping responses and emerge stronger or will adopt debilitating responses and emerge worse off for the experience. There is a limited period of time during which the individual is open to change and during which effective options are available before the crisis escalates or the individual adopts an ineffective response such as acting out or withdrawing. These facts mean that crisis intervention must be available at the time of crises as opposed to at the time of prearranged appointments. This means 24-hour services that emphasize time-limited interventions without the luxury of extensive background information or exploratory interventions. The crisis worker must be a transitional figure who may initially be quite active and directive, but who must emphasize the competency of the client and seek to mobilize his or her coping responses. Workers must think on their feet and make immediate decisions with limited information and, particularly in telephone situations, limited feedback. In addition, because of the demand for immediate response, crisis workers must also perform with little or no ongoing supervision or feedback.

In summary, the job of crisis intervention demands an individual who is fully prepared to respond immediately to a wide variety of nonselected clients and situations. The worker must respond as an independent helper who has less opportunity for review and data gathering than in other helping situations. The job calls for an active approach that has as its aim the development of a collaborative relationship with essentially healthy individuals. However, with the current emphasis on deinstitutionalization, crisis workers are more and more called upon also to recognize and respond to increasingly dysfunctional individuals in crisis. This calls for yet another set of skills.

It is clear from this job analysis that crisis intervention training cannot consist solely of inculcating trainees with prescribed interventions which apply to particular cases or clients. Rather, the training must develop *problem solvers*—people who can think creatively and independently on their feet. What is more, such people must be able to engage in this problem solving in a wide variety of stressful situations, while resisting the temptation to become *gurus* to confused individuals in crisis. This calls for considerable ego strength as well as an awareness of one's own areas of weakness, concerns, and needs. The training must provide opportunities for development of these awarenesses and must teach individuals to be both active and collaborative with clients.

Training Contents

While crisis workers must be problem solvers in a variety of situations, they are by no means without guidelines for their interventions. In addition to Lindemann's (1944) and Caplan's (1964) seminal works, a number of recommended crisis intervention strategies can be found in the literature. There is considerable consensus found in these sources. Based on a review of the crisis intervention literature and the experience of workers in our crisis service, a generic *helping strategy* was developed. This is a 5-step problem-solving approach that has been consistently applicable in our and in other crisis services. It has also served as a useful framework for other interventions, including the consultation process and the role of trainers in our program. The helping strategy is outlined in Table 1.

The strategy in Table 1 is not the sole content of the training program. It serves as an outline or set of guidelines that will help the crisis worker to organize interventions. It has been noted that workers must still be creative problem-solvers in their helping efforts. They must in effect use *themselves*—their knowledge, reactions, capacity to relate, etc. as tools for helping. Thus, in addition to a basic helping strategy, a second focus of training must be the helpers themselves (Brammer, 1973; Kagan, 1975; Klien, 1967; Reiff & Riessman, 1965).

Each helper brings along personal characteristics, some of which will enhance and some of which will interfere with his or her helpfulness. It is important that the worker discover as many of these characteristics as possible before being placed in the actual crisis situation. The training, then, must provide opportunities to explore oneself in an atmosphere that allows for sharing or modifying these characteristics, as is appropriate.

Familiarity with a basic helping strategy and the capacity to monitor and use one's own reactions in the helping situation must be supplemented with another source of guidelines for helping: an understanding of the nature of crises. This includes an understanding of the experience and common responses of people in crisis, and factors that influence the onset, progress, and outcome of crises. Among the helpful interventions in crisis situations are the provision of information to the confused client as to what is and will be happening, and blocking ineffective responses such as withdrawal or denial. It is, therefore, critically important that the crisis worker be thoroughly aware of the dynamics of the crisis situation. Moreoever, it has been our experience that a clear understanding of crises, and par-

Table 1

Helping Strategy for Crisis Intervention

1. *Establish the Relationship:*
   Convey involvement, acceptance
   Reinforce help-seeking
   Invite to work
   Collaborative/Directive, depending on level
      of functioning
   Provide structure

2. *Define the Problem:*
   Define in client's terms
   Explore depth, implications, changeability of concern
   Be specific, and allow open-ended exploration
   Focus on Now and How versus Then and Why
      (help prioritize)
   Check out final definition with client
   Make mutual, explicit contract based on realistic
      expectations for both

3. *Explore Feelings:*
   Acknowledge
   Accept
   Explore implications of feelings
   Why explore them
   When not to deal with them
   Promote hope
   Reduce anxiety
   Reduce denial, blame

4. *Explore Past Coping Attempts:*
   Transition from problem to problem solving
   Take inventory of client's style, internal
      and external resources
   Avoid solutions tried or reexplore those
      prematurely rejected

Table 1 (Continued)

5. *Explore Alternatives and Develop Action Plan:*
    Generate alternatives—collaborative, if
        possible
    Explore consequences
    Explore how feel about alternative
    Get commitment to specific plans
    Rehearse
    Encourage appropriate pacing
    Explain above problem-solving strategy

---

ticularly the experience of the individual in crisis, not only serves as a source of specific information for helpers but stimulates trainees to generate appropriate helping inteventions on their own.

What has been said so far is that an analysis of the task of crisis intervention indicates that trainees can be supplied with a reasonably consensual intervention strategy, and that this strategy serves as a broad outline within which a variety of helping behaviors can be generated from one's use of one's own responses and an understanding of the crisis situation. The application of these helping responses requires the final focus of the training: basic *skills*. These include such generic helping skills as listening, communication, confrontation, and referral skills.

These, then, are the foci or contents of a training program for crisis workers: (a) knowledge of the nature of crises and the experience of persons in crisis, (b) a basic crisis intervention strategy, (c) an awareness of oneself including strengths and weaknesses relevant to helping and the capacity to monitor and use one's responses during crisis intervention, and (d) a mastery of basic helping skills.

TRAINING GOALS

The training program emphasizes active participation of the trainees in mutual exploration and training as opposed to the passive reception of predigested training content. Trainers not only function as instructors, but they also serve as facilitators who encourage exploration, intercommunication, and the development of personal styles among trainees. The necessity for this emphasis is evident from the job demands of the crisis intervention situation: one cannot develop active, autonomous problem-solvers through a process that places trainees in a passive, recipient role.

There are additional reasons for adopting the above training philosophy. In order to be maximally effective and efficient, a training program should model or parallel the interventions that are being taught. Crisis intervention is a *community* approach on both the service delivery and individual helping levels. It involves a decrease in the separation between providers (agencies, helpers, trainers) and consumers (communities, clients, trainees) by drawing upon the resources of the consumers and actively involving them in the resolution of their own concerns. The goal of this approach is to teach problem-solving rather than offer solutions to passive or helpless clients. The provider seeks to become a transitional figure for clients by helping them to recognize and utilize resources in themselves and their environments. The most effective way of teaching this approach and to facilitate transfer from the training to the intervention situation is to model the approach through the training program by encouraging trainees to utilize the resources of the training group as well as the trainers' expertise.

The final rationale for this active approach comes from the training and adult learning literature. The overwhelming consensus in this literature is an indictment of the purely didactic, passive learning approach. The central theme is that adults bring into learning situations considerable experiences that can and should be drawn upon and that they quickly disengage when required to become passive listeners. It has also been found that skills, interventions, or performances can best be learned by *doing* or practice (Bloom, 1956; Egan, 1975; Kagan, 1975; Knowles, 1973).

This active, participatory approach is implemented through the experiential-didactic training technique to be described and by the forging of what has been called the core-group approach (Gorman, 1973; Klien, 1967; Miles, 1973) or the *learning community* (Egan, 1975; Meador & Rogers, 1973). The message given to trainees in this approach is that: (a) each brings important skills and qualities to the training group and that trainees will be learning as much about helping and about persons in crisis from each other as they will from the trainers, and (b) training will be accomplished through inter-active participation and cooperation rather than competition and, therefore, the intent is to establish a norm that allows safe exploration of helping repertoires.

The sense of community is established through strict selection criteria, an initial one day workshop, and the maintenance of "direct, mutual communication" (Ivey, 1974) through clear rules and chan-nels for feedback among trainees and trainers. The reliance on strict selection criteria reinforces the message to trainees that they would not be in the program if they did not have something to offer and encourages them to explore and take risks in training because the emphasis is on developing their skills rather than weeding them out. The workshop and training groups, in addition to covering specific contents, facilitate trainees getting acquainted, and set the tone that encourages them to take risks and try out a variety of behaviors in an effort to develop their own helping styles in a mutual, cooperative framework. It is emphasized that training does not consist of growth or encounter groups, that trainees will not be asked to disclose per-sonal information that they do not wish to, and that only personal characteristics relevant to helping behavior will be explored. Specific rules for helpful, nondefensive feedback are taught and practiced, and written records of feedback from trainers to trainees and vice versa are maintained in open files. Feedback is focused on explicit, behaviorally defined competencies necessary for effective helping. As in any competency-based program, each trainee can proceed at his or her own pace, although the reality demands of staffing a crisis service will impose limits on the amount of time that can be invested in training an individual candidate.

A final point should be addressed concerning what appears to be a dilemma presented by this training philosophy. That is, on the one hand, trainees are told that they must learn to think on their feet, develop a personal helping style, and use *themselves* as a helping instru-ment. On the other hand, they are presented with an explicit and con-sistent set of strategies derived from the crisis literature and the experience of the trainers. On a conceptual level, the apparent con-tradiction between encouraging trainees to find a personal style while following a specific helping strategy may be resolved by Ivey's (1974) distinction between intention and action. Ivey contended that an aim of training is to develop *intentional individuals* who are clearly aware of their intentions and can translate those intentions into behaviors (actions) that can: (a) effectively carry out the intent, and (b) can be altered on the basis of feedback from the environment. Ivey notes that "A central part of growth is intentionality, the blending of intent and behavior, thought and action" (1974, p. 181). In this training program, the helping model represents the proper *intention* (effective helping strategy), and the trainee's personal style represents the action (the individual's way of carrying out that intention in a congruent style). On a programmatic level, the task of the training program then becomes one of clearly presenting the intervention models and then providing the appropriate atmosphere, opportunity for practice, and helpful feedback that facilitate the development of trainees' style.

TRAINING FORMATS

Two basic formats are employed in the training program. One consists of an *instructional sequence* recommended by Gagne (1970) for ensuring acquisition and performance of desired behaviors, and the second is an *experimental* or laboratory approach (Joyce & Weil, 1972) designed to prompt trainees to evolve their own strategies. These formats will be described in detail because it is felt that they most effectively fulfill the training requirements revealed by the task analysis of crisis intervention. That is, crisis workers must be trained to both respond creatively to novel situations and overlearn recommended interventions.

The instructional sequence that is used to teach specific skills or strategies contains the following elements: (a) clear specification of the skill; e.g., a brief lecture and/or tape identifies the given skill and gives the rationale and objective for the skill, (b) modeling of the skill; e.g., trainers give examples and demonstrations of the skill, and trainees model skills for each other in role plays, (c) practice; e.g., skills are practiced primarily through role plays, (d) feedback; e.g., trainer and trainees provide verbal and written feedback to one another, and (e) practice; e.g., continued role plays, supervised counseling, and inservice training.

This format would be used to teach skills or strategies that are generally agreed to be important parts of a crisis worker's repertoire such as the use of open-ended questions or the assessment of lethality in a suicidal situation. Such competencies must be *overlearned*, not simply introduced, because in the tense, fast-paced crisis situation, responses at the top of the helper's repertoire will tend to dominate. The central elements of this instructional sequence are role plays and feedback.

Role Play

Considerable data exist supporting the efficacy of role playing as a training or behavior change technique (Carkhuff, 1969; Corsini, 1966; Day, 1977). The spontaneity and subjective reality (veridicality) generated by role plays allow trainees to practice skills and develop helping styles in a situation that closely approximates the actual counseling experience. At the same time, trainees can experiment and work through errors without the concern for possible harmful effects that such errors might produce with actual clients. The trainer can dictate the type of client role that is presented. This allows tailoring of the training experience to individual trainee's needs and provides a standard stimulus on which to compare trainees for evaluative purposes. By playing both counselors and clients, trainees can experience the helping relationship from both sides. Playing a client can particularly help the trainee develop empathy for clients.

Role playing in a small group and receiving feedback from group members provide the trainee with a variety of reactions to his or her style and skills. This provides important preparation for the actual counseling situation in which the helper must deal with a variety of clients but does not receive clear feedback as to their different reactions. This group setting also allows trainees to observe others and practice listening and feedback skills and present them with a variety of models of helping approaches.

Finally, role playing is considered an effective training technique because it contains many characteristics that maximize generalizability or transfer of training to the actual helping situation: (a) *Identical elements*. The above characteristics, such as spontaneity, coupled with the opportunity to control the type of presenting problem, permit many of the elements of a wide variety of counseling situations to be reproduced, (b) *Overlearning*. Skills are specified and can be practiced beyond mastery until they become a part of the trainees' congruent helping style. The group setting also allows for vicarious practice through observation, (c) *Stimulus variability*. The variety of roles, role players, and reactions from peers will increase the probability of overlap with actual helping situations and clients, (d) *General principles*. The rationale for the use of specific techniques (e.g., open-ended questions) and strategies (e.g., dealing with feelings) is clearly explained, and the introduction, demonstration, and summaries in each training session are all explicitly related to general helping principles, and (e) *Positive performance feedback*. Feedback is a central component of the training program.

In the training session, role plays are chosen to test for a particular skill (e.g., clarifying) or counseling strategy (e.g., exploring feelings), or to provide the trainee with practice in dealing with a particular type of client (e.g., angry or manipulative). Trainees are asked to volunteer to role play in order to obtain practice in an area in which they feel weak, or the trainer chooses a role player because it appears that a trainee needs practice in a given area.

Role players are provided with warmup rehearsals for their roles. While brief, the rehearsals should be conducted almost as a guided fantasy in order to place the trainee *into* the role. After the initial prompting by the trainer, the trainee should report his or her current situation and feelings in present, first person terms. After the role plays, role players are provided with time to readjust from the roles back to the training setting.

Feedback

The process of giving and receiving feedback is an integral component of training as well as of helping. It is through feedback that an individual can discover how well behavior, as perceived by others, corresponds to intentions. Appropriate feedback is an important part of the direct, mutual communication (Ivey, 1974) that is necessary for effective training and helping.

In order for feedback to be appropriate and helpful it must have certain characteristics. An individual receiving feedback and made to feel personally attacked or threatened will naturally become defensive. The more defensive one becomes, the less able or willing one is to accurately perceive the message of the sender. The less defensive one is, the more able one is to concentrate on the content and cognitive meaning of the message. Being observed and receiving feedback on one's behavior is threatening under the best of circumstances and cannot help but result in the receiver feeling anxious. By structuring feedback in a helpful manner, this threat is substantially reduced and the opportunity for the receiver to be open to hearing and accepting feedback is enhanced. The receiver will also be more apt to try out new ideas and be more spontaneous in developing an effective helping style if he or she feels those observing are doing so with an attitude of understanding and a desire to help rather than criticize.

It is not the feedback giver's responsibility to make a judgment as to how "good" or "bad" the peer's performance was, but rather to express the impact of the peer's specific interventions. The guidelines for feedback are followed in order to provide feedback on specific behaviors that can be modified or maintained. For example, in a training group, telling an individual that he or she "was helpful," or "did a good job" or "was too directive" or "condescending," does not tell one what to *do* or avoid doing in order to be helpful. How does one "do a good job" or "be less condescending" the next time? On the other hand, telling a person that his or her consistent eye contact and calm voice tone were perceived as helpful because they helped to assure the client, identifies behaviors that can be practiced and maintained in the person's repertoire.

The job of the feedback giver is to structure the feedback in such a way that the person receiving it can hear it in the most objective and least distorted way possible, and understand it and choose to use it or not use it (Hansen, 1965). Giving helpful feedback is a skill that can be learned and for which specific guidelines are available (Hansen, 1965; Kalafat, Note 1).

Experimental Exercise

As was mentioned previously, a training program should include an experiential approach in addition to an instructional sequence. Rogers (1961) first posited that he was most helpful to the extent that he could directly experience his client's world. Likewise, we have found that when we have been able to create in trainees the experience of persons in crisis, they have been able to generate a variety of appropriate helping responses on their own. Kagan (1975) has described this training process as one of drawing appropriate responses out of trainees rather than putting responses into a repertoire that was assumed to be lacking.

Approaching the concept of experience on a more literal level, if we examine the *content* of the experience of the veteran helper, we find that this experience is made up of an accumulation of direct, in vivo understandings of crisis situations (i.e., clients' concerns and responses as well as the helper's reactions and responses). It is the accumulation and incorporation of these direct experiences that make the veteran helper effective. Now, if at least some portions of these accumulated experiences can be made available to trainees prior to actual client contact, their effectiveness will be enhanced without having used actual clients as fodder for their learning experience. Therefore, the primary characteristics or goals of experimental training are to *distill* the experience of a client in crisis or of a helper responding to crisis situations and present this to the trainee in an evocative way that pulls for affective and instrumental responses.

In order for experiential training to be a true learning experience it must possess additional characteristics (Joyce & Weil, 1972; Schein & Bennis, 1965). The experience must be presented in a relatively ambiguous situation that contains few guidelines for solutions. This forces the trainees to rely on their own resources rather than look to the trainer or an established formula for the appropriate responses. Individual reactions to the experience will serve as a guide for helpful responses.

This lack of structure creates a period of confusion (an "unfreezing" of old responses that can be anxiety-arousing; hence, another component of experiential training must be psychological safety which permits the trainee to take personal risks in evolving a helpful repertoire. This safety is ensured by the group cohesion (learning community), feedback rules, and commitment to avoid irrelevant personal disclosure.

Moreover, trainees will be assuming the dual roles of participant and observer in the learning experience, roles they must assume as helpers. Thus, there must be a procedure for providing a cognitive or intellectual framework for the experience. The group and trainer must process the experience and fit it into an intentional helping framework for each trainee. Again, this process parallels one of the tasks of crisis intervention: helping the client process a confusing experience and gain a cognitive grasp of what may have been an overwhelming situation (Taplin, 1971).

In summary, this approach involves the creation in the trainee of a particular experience such as that of a client in crisis or of a helper dealing with a difficult client, and the creation of a problem for the trainee involving an ambiguous situation which contains no clear instructions or guidelines for solution. The trainee, using the experience created by the exercise as a guide, must develop a strategy or solution to the situation. Thus, the trainee evolves and practices a problem solving strategy. The ambiguous situation with no clear-cut rules or structure makes it difficult to fall back on usual routines and ideas and promotes the development of innovative strategies and, ultimately, a personal helping style.

What is being recommended here is a generic training strategy that is best used in combination with a more structured approach such as the instructional sequence described earlier. That is, if one wishes to teach individuals a given approach such as responding to the panic response of a person overwhelmed in a crisis, an important part of that training is to simulate that situation and require the trainee to respond. An even more effective training device is to place the trainee in the role of the client in these situations as a means of generating helping responses. We feel that responses learned from this direct experiencing will be more congruent and generalized than those taught through passive shaping of overt behavior (e.g., helpful verbal responses) or an intellectual grasp of crisis intervention.

CONCLUSION

The analysis of the job demands of crisis intervention has produced recommendations for training contents, goals, and formats. It should be noted that, while not exclusively, training goals and process have been emphasized over training content. Detailed training contents have not been listed because it is felt that readers can provide their own recommended content, such as specific helping skills to be learned. These will vary somewhat depending on the particular setting and preferences or biases of the trainers.

The attempt here has been to provide useful training formats and strategies that can be adapted to teach a variety of crisis skills and approaches. Thus, if one wishes to teach appropriate interventions for drug or suicidal crises or teach rape counseling or telephone counseling skills, one can carry out a task analysis in one's own setting and/or can draw from sources in the literature (e.g., Lester & Brockopp, 1973; Resnick & Ruben, 1975; Kalafat, Note 1). It is recommended, however, that these contents be taught using an active, participatory approach that involves both an instructional sequence and experiential exercises.

Reference Note

1. Kalafat, J. Training human service workers: Skills, strategy and self. Unpublished manual, 1979.

References

Bloom, B. S. *Taxonomy of educational objectives: Handbook one: Cognitive domain.* New York: David McKay, 1956.

Brammer, L. M. *The helping relationship: Process and skills.* Englewood Cliffs, New Jersey: Prentice-Hall, Inc., 1973.

Caplan, G. *Principles of preventive psychiatry.* New York: Basic Books, 1964.

Carkhuff, R. R. *Helping and human relations* (Vol. 1 & 2). New York: Holt, Rinehart & Winston, Inc., 1969.

Corsini, R. J. *Roleplaying in psychotherapy: A manual.* Chicago: Aldine Publishing Co., 1966.

Day, P. R. *Methods of learning communications skills.* New York: Pergamon Press, 1977.

Egan, G. *The skilled helper: A model for systematic helping and interpersonal relating.* Monterey, California: Brooks/Cole Publishing Co., 1975.

Gagne, R. M. *The conditions of learning.* New York: Holt, Rinehart & Winston, Inc., 1970.

Gorman, A. H. *The leader in the group.* New York: Bureau of Publications, Teachers College, Columbia University, 1973.

Hansen, J. C. Trainees' expectations of supervision in the counseling practicum. *Counselor Education and Supervision,* 1965, *4,* 75-80.

Ivey, A. E. Microcounseling and media therapy: State of the art. *Counselor Education and Supervision,* 1974, *3,* 174-183.

Joyce, B., & Weil, M. *Models of teaching.* Englewood Cliffs, New Jersey: Prentice Hall, Inc., 1972.

Kagan, N. Influencing human interaction-eleven years with IPR. *The Canadian Counselor,* 1975, *9,* 74-97.

Klemp, G. O. *Competency-based training.* Boston: McBer & Co., 1980.

Klemp, G. O., & Spencer, L. M. *Job-competence assessment.* Boston: McBer & Co., 1980.

Klien, W. L. Training human service aides. In E. L. Cowen, E. A. Gardner, & M. Zax, (Eds.), *Emergent approaches to mental health problems.* New York: Appleton-Century-Crofts, 1967.

Knowles, M. *The adult learner: A neglected species.* Houston: Gulf Publishing Co., 1973.

Lester, D., & Brockopp, G. W. *Crisis intervention and counseling by telephone.* Springfield, Ill: Charles C. Thomas Publishers, 1973.

Lindemann, E. Symptomatology and management of acute grief. *American Journal of Psychiatry,* 1944, *101,* 141-148.

Meador, B. D., & Rogers, C. R. Client-centered therapy. In R. J. Corsini (Ed.), *Current psychotherapies.* Itasca, Ill. F. E. Peacock Publishers, Inc., 1973.

Miles, M. B. *Learning to work in groups.* New York: Teachers College Press, Columbia University, 1973.

Reiff, R., & Riessman, F. The indigenous nonprofessional: A strategy of change in community action and community mental health programs. *Community Mental Health Journal,* 1965, *1,* (Monograph).

Resnik, H. L. P., & Ruben, H. L. *Emergency psychiatric care: The management of mental health crises.* Bowie, MD.: The Charles Press Publishers, Inc., 1975.

Rogers, C. R. *On becoming a person.* Boston: Houghton Mifflin Co., 1961.

Schein, E. A., & Bennis, W. G. *Personal and organizational change through group methods.* New York: John Wiley & Sons, 1965.

Taplin, J. R. Crisis theory: Critique and reformulation. *Community Mental Health Journal,* 1971, *1,* 13-23.

Chapter 4

A TRAINING/CONSULTATION MODEL OF CRISIS INTERVENTION WITH LAW ENFORCEMENT OFFICERS

Clyde A. Crego
Marilyn Wendland Crego

This chapter presents a model for training law enforcement officers as crisis interveners. The model is based on a number of basic concepts and training principles. These include an application of general adult learning principles to the specific needs and characteristics of the law enforcement officer, a training model based on a consultation process, and an emphasis on experiential learning. These concepts and principles are applied specifically in this chapter to the development of crisis intervention skills. A specific training/consultation program is described in some detail.

It is widely known that police officers provide a variety of human services, including dealing with persons in crisis (Goldstein, Monti, Sardino, & Green, 1979). The role of the police officer in the area of crisis intervention is now so widely accepted that there is little evaluation being conducted of the form and/or appropriateness of this role (Kobetz, 1974). To be sure, the increasing official use being made of police officers in situations requiring specialized human relations skills is consistent with community-based mental health services programming in general.

Utilization of all appropriate resources in alleviation of distress in individuals has resulted in an increase in the number of crisis intervention training programs for police officers (Crego, Note 1). At the same time, much of the programming for this function, and the subsequent training for it, has occurred in a rather isolated way, typically without regard to: (a) the unique role of police in crisis situations, (b) consultation models that emphasize planning for normal crisis intervention role development in police, and (c) evaluation and follow-up strategies aimed at maximizing actual on-the-job utilization of crisis skills by officers (Crego, Note 2).

Currently, a number of specialized programs are offered to police officers in many types of skill development and self-help workshop paradigms. Assertion training, interviewing skills, stress management, and assessment centers represent but a few of these trends in the modern continuing education of police. The complex role of the officer and its often confusing, if not seemingly incompatible, requirements highlights the need for such programs. However, it appears that much of the training, particularly in skill development areas, is offered on a random basis to "volunteer" officers (Crego, Crego & Mason, Note 3). Little needs-assessment work precedes programming done for specific, job-related learning objectives being established by either the police administrative staff or the participants themselves.

At a time when excellent human skills training is available, it would seem that the appropriateness and effective utilization of such training would be enhanced through employment of a training/consultation model aimed at meeting the specific and realistic needs of police officers whose roles necessitate the application of psychological skills in a deliberate fashion. Attention to police organizational needs as well as to the needs of specific officers is also warranted in an investment of human skills training. This is consistent with models employing participatory management as well as participant involvement in training program development.

Another trend in human skills development programs results from the special learning formats developed for adult learners which attend to their unique learning needs (Houle, 1980). Nonetheless, crisis training programs for police have often neglected to utilize the current state-of-the-art principles of adult learning. The posttraining use of specific crisis intervention skills by police is related to the extent to which the training utilized what is known about the adult learner, as will be discussed in the next section.

Planning for utilization of police in human services roles is seen to depend on a consultation model that takes into consideration the role needs, potential role-development areas, and specific behavioral and attitudinal attributes required for effective use of police as crisis interveners. A process consultation model can facilitate the ongoing application of expanded role models in a police environment where multiple role pressures and responsibilities frequently conflict with the increasing use of human service skills by police. Second, a training model linked to what is known about a specific department's needs for consultation is likely to be more successful than a training model that does not account for the work environment in which new skills are to be employed. Third, effective training should be based on sound learning objectives, needs assessment for individual trainees, principles of adult learning, follow-up evaluation, and principles of crisis intervention skill development that are consistent with the more general role of the modern police officer.

Fourth, the need for an integrated consultation/training model arises from the fact that police trainers too often develop programs that do not consider organizational context variables such as selection of trainees, process for posttraining application of skills, and relevant departmental dynamics. In addition, many training programs are utilized for inappropriate reasons. For example, police administrators may send low performance officers to skill development programs with the unspoken aim of getting these officers sub rosa counseling. Failure to obtain police officer input into the planning of training programs may result in a failure in the transfer-of-training process.

Failure on the part of trainers to assess and understand the specific learning styles of police officers in general, and their trainees in particular, may also result in a failure of later transfer-of-training. Police who do not perceive the learning model as appropriate to their needs may either discard the acquired skills later or fail to learn them in the first place. An adult learning model emphasizing participant involvement in deciding what gains are to be made in training and in skills application on-the-job is more likely to produce skills acquisition and posttraining utilization.

A consultation/training model systematically integrating the features described is expensive in terms of time needed to develop it properly for any specific use. However, such a model is not necessarily expensive monetarily if individual police officers are permitted to participate in the planning phases of the program's development; nor is such a model expensive in its long-term benefits.

It is proposed that a model for developing crisis intervention skills (and skills utilization) in police officers: (a) employ carefully executed consultation which results in training programs developed specifically to meet the needs of that department—as opposed to isolated, nonspecific, and unrelated programs, and (b) take into account the police officer as an adult learner having unique attributes and learning needs in relation to specific sets of skills.

Use of this integrated consultation/training model is not restricted to the development of crisis intervention skills in police, but may also be employed in other skills development areas in which police are currently being trained by human services specialists.

The model is a 3-part one:

1. The use of consultation processes in establishing program needs and elements

2. The actual training itself

3. The use of continued consultation in a police department to:

   (a) insure skill application and continued skills development
   (b) evaluate the learning

Following a discussion of the characteristics of the law enforcement officer as an adult learner, this model will be described in detail.

THE LAW ENFORCEMENT OFFICER AS AN ADULT LEARNER

Several general characteristics of the police officer as an adult learner are relevant to the consultation/training program model.

First, human personality growth can be seen as moving from a position of dependence to one of self-awareness and self-direction. Adult learners therefore need to be involved in a self-diagnosis of their learning needs; they need as well to view learning not as a passive/dependent situation, but as a shared responsibility between themselves and their trainers.

Second, an adult's accumulation of life experience becomes a significant resource in a new learning situation and should be actively and intentionally used in planning specific training for individuals. Adults can contribute more to the learning of their peers, providing the basis for much more productive use of group learning formats than is frequently true with young learners. Adults can relate and apply new knowledge more readily to concrete situations. One disadvantage imposed by this experience-accumulation is that adult learners are frequently set in their learning styles and more resistant to new concepts because of habits established over the years. New learning situations must first free them from their preconceptions and fixed patterns of thought.

Third, the adult learner's time perspective changes from childhood to adulthood, from postponed application of knowledge to immediacy of application—from subject-centered to problem-centered learning.

These concepts are valuable in understanding the adult learner in general, but do not describe the specific variables or characteristics of law enforcement officers. These characteristics vary from department to department, depending on department size and the selection techniques and types of training utilized by specific departments (Crego, Note 4).

A first consideration is the wide variety of motives and goals characterizing any group of training program participants. Some common ones are as follows. First, there are those participants who are required to attend. While this does not necessarily predict a poorly functioning participant, it usually does result in attendees who are not initially engaged in the learning process. A second group are those who attend training sessions with personal goals of career progression/advancement. For example, newly appointed squad commanders would represent such a group. In most instances, the largest group will have job enhancement goals—goals of improving their day-to-day performance, and consequently a practical "how to" orientation. Most workshop groups will also have a few participants with assorted other motives such as curiosity, a paid day off, or an opportunity to meet old friends. In a heterogeneous group such as described, it is clear that trainers are faced with various participant goals, expectations, and learning agenda, and must find a way to engage the group, as a group, in spite of this diversity.

Two additional considerations that have been found to be particularly important in programming for law enforcement officers are those of cognitive interest and past experience. With regard to cognitive interest, it is the *interest* factor that seems so significant, not cognitive ability alone. In training police the authors have observed a bipolar distribution along this dimension. The authors have worked with many officers who are highly cognitively oriented in the sense of a curiosity about psychological theory and searching for an understanding of why certain skills and techniques are effective or ineffective, although they may not have the standard psychological language for articulating this. It would be a mistake, therefore, to aim training only at the practical "how to" (nonconceptual) individuals, and it is critical to alert the group to the dual goals of skill development and understanding at the beginning of a training program. Both situation (problem-centered) and content-centered learning need to be included in the training model.

A second consideration found to be significant in police programming is the extent to which the individual participants generalize from their past experience. This seems to be limited in many adult learners. They can apply learnings, but often underestimate what they already know or have experienced from other situations. The effect is that they feel unnecessarily like a novice in new situations. The issue seems not to be one of ability to generalize, but rather of willingness to risk—a self-concept issue. This has two implications for the trainer. First, the trainer must be aware of this tendency to underestimate and undervalue pretraining skills and abilities. Second, the training needs to directly incorporate opportunities for the learners to discover and more fully utilize these existing skills and abilities. Both aspects will be articulated more specifically in the description of the training program.

Another issue found to be especially significant for trainers is that of the multiple roles characterizing police activities. In any given on-the-job situation, an officer may be involved in an investigation, collecting and recording information, relating to his or her partner, dealing with the emotions of a victim, and insuring the officer's own safety. This multiplicity of roles and the potential role conflict it generates is, the authors believe, something frequently overlooked and misunderstood by nonpolice trainers.

Police trainees frequently criticize training programs for not adequately understanding the complexity and multiplicity of their on-the-job roles. For instance, police roles tend to be highly action-oriented and focused on outcomes and on "doing." As a result, officers tend to be oriented toward quickly moving through psychological processes and to undervalue the significance of other forms of help-giving, such as listening. Consequently, they frequently need to be convinced of the importance of a developmental approach to working with people, and the value of their role in that process.

Law enforcement officers have greatly expanded their perception of their role in recent years (Kobetz, 1974). Nonetheless, it is not uncommon for police to question the value of interpersonal skills training, or to actively reject it; some officers equate interpersonal skills and functions with "softness" and assume that they interfere with their other roles as a police officer.

Two final issues about police officers as adult learners merit comment. These concern the officer/participant's expectations about a training program. First, the expectation that a workshop or seminar is a lecture and "sit-and-listen" event is common. Many potential participants may not be familiar with an experiential format which involves them in the process of training. This may be clearly threatening to some, as it risks exposure of one's level of expertise to peers and in some cases to superiors. Early establishment of an attitude that training for crisis intervention skills involves "trying out" and "experimenting" may help, but the threat still exists for many.

Second, there is a common expectation that the psychologist-trainer will present himself or herself as the expert and the police officer as the beginner and, in addition, hold stereotypes about police trainees as poor learners because of their concrete thinking, or anti-intellectualism. Such attitudes, subtly conveyed, can have a tremendous impact on whether the trainers will be perceived as facilitators or merely critical evaluators. Understanding the role complexity of police officers' work and valuing the skills they already have and use daily is, it is believed, essential to successfully engage trainees in a training experience.

Consultation/Training Model

A major difficulty many adult learning/training programs have encountered results from lack of effective prior planning (Cope & Gaydos, 1978). Elements of prior planning include establishing the purposes of training at an agency or departmental level (including needs assessment), the development of police administrative input into creating role/skill utilization strategies, and insuring suitable trainee selection procedures. Departmental support of the training activities is needed to obtain maximal training materials, feasible scheduling of training sessions, suitable physical space, and support staff for the trainers. Other writers have pointed out that failure to build in "nuts and bolts" support for training usually leads to failure in the training program (Cope & Gaydos, 1978). Those writers have suggested the use of a planning committee to implement training program needs following the establishment of departmental commitment to the training process. The planning committee may be utilized to formulate the objectives of the workshop in specific terms, and can be utilized in the design of the evaluation procedures to be used in assessing the learning objectives.

Departmental objectives may be established through consultation with senior administrators, training officers, middle-management responsible for "street" and "patrol" assignments, and via a needs assessment instrument administered to officers working in situations requiring the frequent utilization of crisis intervention skills. A process model of consultation may be applied in engaging departmental personnel in participating in the evaluation of the need for a training program, similar to the model for mediated services suggested by Paul (1979). The establishment of the planning committee should be designed to insure committee member investment in the outcome of the training sessions themselves *and* in the development of a posttraining strategy for insuring opportunity to use the skills on-the-job, obtaining officer feedback, and creating as well as maintaining support mechanisms for continuing learning. In addition, evaluating the learning objectives several months following training is an important evaluation tool.

In departments of sufficient size, selection of a pilot-training group is recommended. Trainers, as members of the planning committee, will be able to modify elements of the training program to fit the unique needs a particular department may have in relation to the learning and implementation of crisis intervention skills.

Consultation as the first stage of training program planning is most effective when trainers have some familiarity with police functions and officer attributes. It is the authors' experience that many experienced, usually well-qualified "outside" trainers underestimate the preexisting interpersonal skills and potential learning capacities of police personnel. This is obviously detrimental to the aims of a sound training program. At the same time, human services trainers who work frequently with police have been appropriately criticized by senior police administrators for identifying too strongly with police roles and functions (Crego, Note 2). Such role confusion in the trainer can result in loss of the objectivity necessary for effective facilitation.

Following consultation and conjoint planning of the training program by police officers and the trainers, a training program utilizing a skill development paradigm is effective in meeting the needs of most officers. A model that is both experiential and didactic should result in learning and the transfer of new skills to the work setting.

A learning model that begins by emphasizing the trainee-participant's own experiences and concepts quickly establishes an adult learning mode that permits not only an expansion of existing skills, but also enhances nondefensive learning of new skills. Including participants in the design of early phases of the learning process establishes credibility quickly and identifies skills to be worked on which have the highest chance to be implemented on-the-job by individuals "owning" these particular skills.

A Suggested Training Program

The following describes a training program based on the theoretical principles so far discussed. The objectives of the training program are met by a carefully designed sequence of experiences (exercises), both didactic and practice-oriented. The program is designed for a consecutive 3-day training period. The program must be staffed for didactic sessions, small group practice and discussion sessions (four to six trainees), and individual feedback opportunities. A team of three trainers is optimum for a group of 14 to 18 trainees.

Phase I

Exercise 1: The first exercise is conducted in a small group format in which participants are asked to "brainstorm" relevant situations that police encounter requiring the use of crisis intervention. This exercise is conducted in 15 to 20 minutes. A leader makes a list on large news print of the situations the group identifies as relevant. This exercise accomplishes several things, in that it: (a) serves as a participant "warm up," (b) establishes participant input and "agenda" immediately, (c) establishes a beginning rationale for why the skills are being learned, and (d) provides direct evidence that the trainers value participants' views of their training needs and that the program will be planned to take those needs into account.

Police officers will generate, via brainstorming, many varied kinds of situations from their own direct or indirect (peer) experiences. They are usually situation rather than skill-centered in their own thinking. Initiating exercises that focus on the *participant's* perspective of human crisis facilitates rapid involvement from as many participants as possible.

It is important that trainers understand that the above aims of such exercises follow established principles of adult learning as described in a previous section. Developing aspects of the skills-content to be practiced in training from the participants themselves engages them in the process of being an active learner, rather than a passive participant.

Exercise 2: This exercise involves a second brainstorming task in which the participants are asked to brainstorm the many functional roles they must engage in as officers. The trainer stresses the importance of viewing their job as involving multiple, complex roles and priorities at any given time or perhaps for any given situation.

From the list of crisis situations developed in Exercise 1, participants are then asked to generate a list of skills needed for performing in these situations. Most groups of trainees can produce a very comprehensive list of the appropriate skills needed. Although highly verbal groups may generate extensive lists, 10 to 15 skill items usually provide more than sufficient content for a 3-day workshop.

Exercise 3: A key next step is to ask the participants to self-assess themselves on each of the skills or role-elements developed from the preceding exercise. Self-ratings on two separate dimensions are useful: (a) skill level, and (b) comfort level.

Providing the participants with feedback about their self-ratings increases their awareness of areas they may have difficulty with, or about which they wish to receive further training. Participants are asked to share their self-ratings in small groups facilitated by one of the trainers. The mutual sharing among participants and feedback provided by the trainer serve two purposes, in that they: (a) establish a learning (as opposed to evaluative) atmosphere and thus reduce anxiety, and (b) begin the process of helping trainees differentiate the aspects of skills they wish to practice and enable them to make decisions about doing so in later exercises.

Transfer of training from the educational program to the job setting is an obvious, but difficult to attain goal in all structured programs of this type. We believe that the beginning sequence of exercises outlined above is necessary prior to training in crisis intervention itself, in order for transfer of learning to occur.

Phase II

The next phase of the training program can be labelled an "input phase." At this point, the participants acquire information about crisis intervention itself. Three types of information are presented in formal fashion to the trainees: (a) information about crisis, stages of crisis, and attributes of persons in crisis, (b) information about the process of crisis intervention, and (c) information about the actual skills employed in crisis intervention work.

In addition to providing much of the traditional information about the nature of crisis and crisis intervention, it is also important to include the following information: (a) psychological changes persons in crisis undergo, (b) concepts of "developmental change" and stages of adulthood, (c) kinds of learning that occur *during* a crisis, and (d) crisis behavior (not necessarily focusing on psychopathological behavior).

Exercise 4: The first didactic session may be followed by an exercise in which the participants are presented "real life" crisis situations as stimulus material. The group task involves determining the *limits* of the crisis intervention to be employed in the context of: (a) the problem itself, and (b) police officer role limitations.

Helping participants understand the difference between immediate crisis alleviation and long-term problem-resolution is an important task to be accomplished at this time in training. Helping participants understand the stages of crisis does not imply that police trainees should intervene at all of these stages. We have found that it is especially important to help police trainees understand how to deal with the immediate psychological state of a person in crisis.

Phase III

In employing a training model that depends upon self-assessment of trainee interpersonal skills, it is useful to develop a set of exercises incorporating basic helping skills used in counseling psychology. For example, a stage model of the helping process aids trainees in acquiring a strong perception that helping is a stage-like process, and that the skills involved at each stage are consistent with the skills found to work most effectively at the various stages of crisis as well.

The elementary model to be introduced at this point has three helping stages: (a) listening, (b) assessment/understanding, and (c) action/responding. The basic concepts and skills involved in these helping behaviors are explained to the participants.

Exercise 5: In introducing this exercise, the trainer provides examples of trainee-generated crisis situations from Exercise 1. This may be done via the use of human models who role play the appropriate skills associated with listening, understanding, and action for the situation being demonstrated. The task is for participants to observe the models for the skills being employed by the trainer/intervener. This task also involves clarifying for the trainee the helping process and what is to be learned about the specific skills involved.

Exercise 6: The training group is asked to practice these previously observed skills including ineffective skills. This is accomplished by dividing the participants into triads in which one member functions as the person in crisis, the second the intervener, and the third member serves as observer. The full training group selects a crisis situation for all triads to role play. Trainers must insure that the situations are not too difficult to permit successful skill practicing by the intervener. Each member of each triad should take turns in each role.

Following a trainer-imposed time limit in the exercise, (typically 1 hour), all triads are asked to reconvene as a group for a report on how each group performed the skills. Intensive feedback is provided by the trainees serving as the crisis-person about their experience with the intervention, how they perceived it, what it felt like, etc. This type of *peer* (and direct experiential) feedback provides information, aids in conceptualizing appropriate skill utilization for particular crisis and helping stages, and helps prepare the trainees further for learning in an experiential and peer feedback mode. Trainer feedback is also given to the triad role players at this time.

In the group discussion the trainers focus on helping participants respond to the question, "How can I modify my own responses?" By regularly clarifying the helping concepts from the model and by focusing discussion on the *skills* being practiced and learned, the learners will become increasingly aware of the concepts being utilized and of the utility of such concepts in a crisis situation. Appropriate clarification of each concept will aid in retention as well.

Phase IV

Exercise 7: The next exercise involves the use of videotape equipment. The trainees are assigned to dyads in which one person plays the role of a person in crisis while the other trainee serves as intervener. They are provided a suitable situation to role play in a location permitting the trainee to adopt as much as possible an experimental attitude towards practicing the skills. Standard videotaping practices are employed, and the tapes are *not* rerun at this time.

Exercise 8: The participants are assigned to work one-to-one with a trainer while the remainder of the group discuss their reactions to the training process in general. In the individual sessions participants are invited to engage in a brief self-evaluation of their work in the prior learning exercises and practice sessions. From the self-evaluation they are in turn asked to establish some individual learning goals in relation to the skills being employed in the model. They are helped in the process by referring back to the original brainstorming material produced in the earlier exercises and self-assessment. Self-evaluation includes questions such as: "What do I do well?", "What do I want to do more effectively?", "How can I get there?" The trainer and trainee then review each tape privately and discuss skills needing modification.

Exercise 9: In this exercise the trainees practice new situations in dyads while being videotaped. This is usually done in small groups and is followed by *immediately* reviewing the tapes with intensive trainer feedback. This feedback may be general in form, but must include as its major component information the trainee can use about the skills he or she chooses to work on.

Phase V

A lecture is given on changes expected in a person in crisis as a result of intervention. The trainer will discuss various types of helping skills that move a person in crisis from one phase of crisis to the next. The trainer may include some specific intervention techniques suitable for dealing with various kinds of crisis such as bereavement. Material is presented concerning the frequently encountered conflict and ambivalence seen in many crisis persons as they begin to more actively confront their difficulty with the aid of another person.

Exercise 10: The training group selects dyads to perform this exercise. Situations are given that will elicit: (a) demands from a crisis person for an action-solution too quickly, and (b) no action. The role playing is videotaped.

The entire group watches the taping and participates in the feedback processing which occurs immediately following the completion of dyad tapings. The group is asked to suggest *changes* in the responses needing such modification.

The trainer then adopts the role of the crisis client. The dyad members who previously role played the intervener are again in that role. The trainer attempts to help the learner/interveners improve their new responses by permitting appropriate change to occur in the role playing.

A repeat of this training exercise is performed until all the participants have had the opportunity to improve their own responses in this fashion.

Phase VI

Exercise 11: The trainers design the next exercise specifically for each participant. This exercise involves the use of specially prepared skill-building sessions in which each participant continues to work on both goals established by him or her and skill-improvement areas highlighted by the previous experience. During these private skill-enhancement sessions the trainees are guided to begin to think more systematically about skills they may wish to practice in their everyday work or life. Examples of these might include learning how to listen in the face of demands for action, coping with intense emotionality in others, and handling extreme psychopathology.

Exercise 12: The training group at this time is asked to brainstorm ideas on "how to transfer" their learning to the posttraining environments to which they will be returning. If the trainees are from a single department, efforts may be made at this time to help them build peer groups designed to facilitate posttraining continued learning. The group is also asked to indicate any unintended learning the training may have promoted and how such "spin-off" might be employed in helping them expand their skills following training.

Evaluation: It is essential that evaluation be completed by participants to provide the trainers with information about program elements that are effective/ineffective for particular types of trainees or trainee groups. Evaluation may include satisfaction measures, but more importantly should make use of *ratings* of actual learning gained. The authors have found it useful to use evaluation forms with items relating to each exercise or program element as well as measures of satisfaction with style, format, instructors, and learning accomplishments. The items ask for perceived previous skill and knowledge level rankings in part "a," followed by a part "b" to the item in which the trainee rates perceived amount of skill and/or knowledge gain.

Asking participants to choose one skill they especially wish to practice on-the-job, writing this down on a card and giving it to the instructor can generate follow-up research three to six months later.

The trainees are asked to respond to questions about their planned practice in addition to other questions about aspects of the training experience which promoted or failed to promote increased effectiveness in utilizing crisis skills.

Exercise 13: The final exercise involves standard team building exercises to aid the officer/trainees in learning how to establish a peer support and feedback system. These exercises will depend in part on whether the participants actually work together. It is helpful if the officers can establish small groups of four to six which can meet on a regular basis to discuss the application of their crisis skills. The trainers work with these small groups during this exercise to help them establish some ground rules for meeting and in identifying issues they wish to receive feedback on in the future. This process will also strengthen the team bonds if the officers are permitted to call on each other for support and mutual assistance when actually engaged in a difficult crisis situation.

POSTTRAINING CONSULTATION

Pretraining consultation will include establishing a commitment from departmental training and administrative officers to participate in the design of mechanisms for facilitating the posttraining utilization of newly gained skills. While this is understandably not an easy task, the employment of officers and their self-selection for tasks often do permit some flexibility in this area. Administrative interest and reinforcement for continuing learning should be utilized to provide "payoff" for the training and continued interest. Involved administrative officers should meet with the trainers following training to receive consultative assistance on how to give feedback and positive reinforcement to officers who effectively attempt to utilize their crisis skills. Instructions on the *continued* need for feedback concerning issues of "burn-out" have been found to be helpful.

Administrative help will be needed to establish an appropriate system for continued peer group meeting, at designated times, in the continuing learning of crisis intervention. Gaining administrative understanding that team building should occur is usually beneficial.

Certainly the planning of a half-day reunion with the training staff to process transfer of learning issues/problems is a most effective way to insure appropriate follow-up practices, and to enhance the participants' own involvement in maintaining both a self-assessment and self-directed movement toward continued development of skills. Inclusion of key departmental administrative staff in these final phases of the program helps insure commitment by the department to the actual ongoing learning of crisis intervention skills, helps provide realistic assessment of officer role potentials and limitations, and stimulates officers who are invested in their own continuing learning.

SUMMARY

The training model described is based on effective consultation and planning as well as principles of education useful in training law enforcement officers to be crisis interveners. The training depends on the use of both trainer and peer feedback, and builds upon participants' self-identified, preexisting interpersonal skills and psychological abilities. The model's effectiveness in training law enforcement officers depends also on the ability of the trainer/consultants to adapt it to a particular department's needs and characteristics. The authors have observed that officers who have completed this training have often been able to more easily transfer their learning to other areas requiring specialized skills, such as in hostage negotiations, although this latter area requires specific training as well.

REFERENCE NOTES

1.   Crego, C. The law enforcement officer as a crisis intervener. Invited Address, FBI Academy National Associates, 1978.
2.   Crego, C. A training/consultation model for law enforcement officers. Paper presented at Annual Convention of American Psychological Association, New York, 1979.

3.   Crego, C., Crego, M. Wendland, & Mason, R. E. Law enforcement agency consultation utilizing skill development programming: A model. Program presented and chaired at Annual Convention of American Psychological Association, New York, 1979.

4.   Crego, M. Wendland. The police officer as an adult learner. Paper presented at Annual Convention of American Psychological Association, New York, 1979.

REFERENCES

Cope, C., & Gaydos, E. *Toward more effective administration in facilities and workshops.* Final Report, H.E.W. Training Grant No. 45, p. 35213/7-01 (1978).

Goldstein, A. P., Monti, P. J., Sardino, T. J., & Green, D. J. *Police crisis intervention.* New York: Pergamon Press, 1979.

Houle, C. O. *Continuing learning in the professions.* San Francisco: Jossey-Bass, 1980.

Kobetz, R. W. *Crisis intervention and the police: Selected readings.* Gaithersburg, Maryland: International Association of Chiefs of Police, 1974.

Paul, S. C. Consultation evaluation: Turning a circus into a performance. In M. K. Hamilton & C. J. Meade, (Eds.), *Consulting on campus.* San Francisco: Jossey-Bass, 1979.

Section II

APPLICATION OF CRISIS
INTERVENTION TECHNIQUES

The concept of crisis intervention ultimately rests upon the observation that persons overwhelmed by stress, whatever its origins, display similar responses and benefit most from similar forms of assistance. The preceding chapters have also shown that there is considerable concurrence regarding the fundamental skills of successful crisis workers. The ability to listen carefully, respond nonjudgmentally, and facilitate problem solving are almost universally accepted as traits to be identified through selection and fostered through training. Yet the broad range of settings and situations in which crisis concepts have been invoked would seem to require a particularization of skills and methods, as well as the application of generic concepts. Each interventive strategy poses specific challenges to the worker and each stressful event is associated with particular risks. A truly sophisticated intervention must consider these variables as well as the commonalities. The following chapters represent attempts at refining general crisis theory by moving beyond general concepts to principles applicable to a particular interventive modality or source of stress.

The focus of Chapter 5, by Karl Slaikeu, is the unique characteristics and job-role demands of telephone interventions. The hot line approach permits a client instant access to the counselor and considerable control over the interaction. Conversely, the worker must enter each contact without prior knowledge of the problem and without access to the tools of influence that are available in prearranged, face-to-face contacts in a professional setting. Neither client nor counselor is aided or encumbered by visual cues. Obviously, the telephone service requires a worker who can rapidly assess intent, problem area, and risk level using only the caller's words and intonations as measures. Further, the counselor must be skilled at verbally conveying feelings and ideas which will encourage the caller to sustain the conversation and reveal relevant information.

Chapter 6, by Kirby, Polak, and Weerts, poses some interesting contrasts to the issues raised by Slaikeu. Kirby et al. apply crisis concepts to a situation where the client is known to be in considerable distress, probably subject to much coercion from others, and enters a situation where the risk of further external control is high. In discussing the client who is literally or figuratively at the door of the psychiatric hospital, these authors are actually examining a case where the potential treatment, i.e., institutionalization, may be regarded as an additional stressor beyond those that engendered the original crisis. Unlike the telephone crisis worker who is hard pressed to gain sufficient control of the contact to be helpful, the hospital screener is challenged to create an opportunity for the client to maintain some control over his or her life. The specific approach advocated by Kirby and his colleagues relies upon removing the client from a family situation which has proven overwhelming, but placing him or her in a reasonably similar family setting where a sense of mastery may be regained. Whereas the telephone counselor may be the first and only source of help, the crisis worker in Kirby's model functions primarily as a change agent who places the client in a restorative environment. Further, the sponsor family which accepts the client is not trained or oriented toward the application of traditional crisis counseling skills. In effect, therefore, Chapter 6 describes a crisis intervention approach where the individual is permitted to escape the locus of stress and avoid the imposition of added stress associated with placement in a threatening and unfamiliar environment, the hospital.

The final three chapters in this section deal with crises where the "stress reduction" strategy cannot be employed because an intensely stressful event with inevitable sequelae has already occurred. In Chapter 7, Rita Yopp Cohen considers the crisis associated with the diagnosis and treatment of major medical problems. In Chapter 8, Franklin discusses responses to the crises produced by natural disasters. Finally, in Chapter 9, Kilpatrick and Veronen examine the effects of rape and the counseling needs of its victims.

The cumulative importance of these chapters lies in the way they demonstrate that different stressors have their own unique impact on the client and require specialized forms of intervention. Cohen, for a first example, looks at the impact of prognostically negative physical disorders where the initial diagnosis represents the preliminary shock, the treatment may pose further threat, and the ultimate risk of death or disability continues to loom over the patient. A need is cited in this case for considerable educational effort to assist the patient to accurately understand his or her condition and its implications. Another relatively novel crisis strategy recommended by Cohen is the formation of groups of similarly affected patients and their families. In part, this latter approach becomes desirable because the crisis precipitant, the disease, is a continuing source of stress rather than a discrete event whose impact may dissipate with time. Franklin, in considering natural disasters, also focuses upon stressors that impact suddenly but involve ''aftershocks.'' He noted that individuals faced by events like earthquakes or floods may initially muster their resources and cope successfully, only to break down later when losses are assessed and rebuilding efforts prove frustrating. A unique feature here is that the on-site crisis workers themselves may be subject to the immediate effects of the chaos and the heavy pressures to provide assistance.

Finally, in Chapter 9, Kilpatrick and Veronen consider the treatment of rape victims, for whom social attitudes are a crucial stressor beyond the impact of the assault itself. The victims of both disease and natural disaster may reasonably rely upon the sympathetic understanding of others; also, they are unlikely to blame themselves for their misfortune. Rape victims, however, experience the trauma of the event and then may face feelings of guilt and contamination on top of the anxieties any uncontrollable painful occurrence may produce. As with Franklin's analysis of disaster reactions, Kilpatrick and Veronen suggest that the full effect of a sexual assault may be felt long after the event, and recovery may be much slower than traditional crisis models suggest. Here again, the unique features of the precipitating event point to the need for a particularized conceptualization and mode of intervention.

Chapter 5

CRISIS INTERVENTION BY TELEPHONE*

Karl A. Slaikeu

Levine and Levine (1970) have documented how helping services are influenced, if not shaped, by the social and economic conditions of the times. This has been no less true of hot line or telephone counseling services than of other social services. Modern telephone crisis intervention, which began in the late 1950s, became the backbone of the suicide prevention movement, and grew rapidly in the context of social activism in the 1960s. Although it was not the first 24-hour telephone counseling service (New York City's National Save-A-Life League established one in 1906), the Los Angeles Suicide Prevention Center is credited with first developing techniques on how to use the telephone to perform lifesaving interventions (McGee, 1974). Its use of volunteer personnel, 24-hour and 365-day a year coverage, and training institutes on how best to counsel distressed callers over the telephone laid the groundwork for the rapid development of centers across the country. While many of the smaller centers folded after a few years, most survived, and a steady rise in the number of centers

*The author wishes to express his appreciation to Dr. Charles Haywood, Director of Crisis Intervention Institute, Buffalo, New York, for providing information concerning Crisis Services, Inc., and for his helpful comments on an earlier draft of this paper.

was seen through 1980. A recent survey of suicide prevention and crisis services in the United States and Canada found over 500 known centers, compared with less than 50 in 1965 (Haywood & Leuthe, Note 1). Moreover, this figure does not include the large number of college based counseling services, youth oriented hot lines, and religious counseling hot lines. In addition to an increase in the number of centers, the 1970s also saw the development of new programs (Motto, 1979) as well as a rapid expansion in the telephone counseling literature (Slaikeu, in press). The net result has been a demonstration of the unique role telephone counseling can play in a comprehensive service delivery system.

The purposes of this chapter are to: (a) provide an overview of theoretical considerations in telephone counseling, (b) describe the chief features (including changes over the past 15 years) of one exemplary service, (c) highlight key evaluation issues, and (d) outline important considerations for the future development of telephone counseling.

CRISIS CONCEPTS AND TELEPHONE INTERVENTION

The major elements of crisis theory have been summarized by a number of writers, each building on the early work of Gerald Caplan (1964). (For example, see Aguilera, Messick, & Farrell, 1974; Baldwin, 1979; Viney, 1976). Life crises are seen as time-limited states of emotional upset and disorganization, characterized chiefly by the breakdown of previously adequate coping mechanisms (Caplan, 1964). The intervention process is viewed as one that should take place *during* the time of disorganization and emotional upset. The assumption is not simply that individuals are most needy at these particular times, although this is certainly true, but also that tremendous opportunities for growth exist during crisis states. Several years ago, Tyhurst (1958) argued that help should be available at this "optimum time," during which the disorganization of the crisis state makes individuals vulnerable (Halpern, 1973) and suggestible (Taplin, 1971). The implication was that, for some people, things indeed had to get worse before they could get better. Crisis intervention aimed at working with people when things were at their worst, with a goal of facilitating reorganization which would be at a higher level of functioning. For many people the crisis state was a time to rework previously unresolved personality issues (Miller & Iscoe, 1963), one route toward converting a traumatic event to an ultimate gain.

The principles of crisis intervention, summarized by a number of writers (e.g., Baldwin, 1979; Butcher & Maudal, 1976; McGee, 1974), are based on the preceding assumptions of crisis theory. Slaikeu (in press) identifies the following characteristics of crisis intervention:

(1) short-term (about one to six sessions);

(2) located close in both time and place to the crisis event (often referred to as "Hansel's Law," McGee, 1974);

(3) focused goals (i.e., resolution of the crisis);

(4) based on assessment of client's strengths as well as weaknesses;

(5) recognition of both the harmful and helpful impacts of social context variables (e.g., family, work, and community variables);

(6) emphasis on multiple subsystems (feelings, thoughts/ expectancies, behavior, physical functioning, interpersonal relationships) in understanding the impact and ultimate resolution of the crisis;

(7) help-oriented to minimize dependency and maximize mastery;

(8) based on active, directive, and flexible therapist behavior.

The use of the telephone requires that telephone counseling consists of more than just the above generic characteristics of crisis intervention. Lester's (1977) summary of the unique characteristics of telephone counseling includes, first of all, increased client control associated with telephone contact. In face-to-face counseling, a client takes a place in the waiting room, perhaps fills out forms or psychological tests given by a receptionist, is ushered into a therapist's office, sits down, and begins talking, all at the guidance or instruction of another person. The length of the contact is usually set, with termination being initiated by the therapist. In telephone counseling, on the other hand, this power differential is equalized. The client not only begins the therapeutic or helping interaction whenever he or she wants to, but is also free to terminate it at any time.

A second feature of telephone counseling is that it preserves client anonymity. The possibility of hiding identity is assumed to facilitate greater self-revelation and openness on the part of many callers.

Third, counselors are also anonymous, which may facilitate the development of positive transference. Visual cues being absent, there is greater opportunity for the counselor to "live up" to the caller's fantasy of what the ideal counselor would be than in a face-to-face situation.

Fourth, telephone counseling reduces the dependency of a caller on an individual counselor, and transfers it to the clinic or counseling service instead. Most callers are asked only for a first name, and dependency on a particular counselor is discouraged.

Fifth, telephone counseling is unique in its accessibility. Most people have a telephone (or ready access to one) and the cost for its use is low. Accessibility is critical for crisis clients, especially those who are suicidal or homicidal, and for those unable to leave their home (e.g., elderly or physically disabled).

Finally, telephone counseling is available at any time, day or night. Most services are open 24 hours a day, year round, which means that assistance is available with a bare minimum of waiting time. (See Miller, 1973, for other properties of telephones pertinent to their use in counseling.)

A number of telephone counseling training programs have been developed during the past 15 years or so. McGee and his colleagues, for example, have distinguished between the teaching of clinical and technical effectiveness (Fowler & McGee, 1973; Knickerbocker & McGee, 1973; McGee, 1974). Clinical effectiveness is based on scales developed by Carkhuff (1969), particularly the measurement of the counselor's ability to demonstrate empathy, warmth, and genuineness to the caller. Technical effectiveness refers to other counselor behavior, including, for example, ability to assess lethality of potential suicide cases, explore resources available to the caller, and make appropriate referrals. Walfish and his colleagues have contributed to the measurement of technical effectiveness by developing a "crisis contracting" scale, which examines counselors' ability to assess the current crisis, explore resources, and develop an action plan on a contractual basis (Walfish, Tapp, Tulkin, Slaikeu, Russell, 1976).

Following a critique of the fragmented nature of existing crisis intervention models, Slaikeu (in press) has proposed a distinction between first and second order crisis intervention. First order intervention, or psychological first aid (PFA), refers to immediate assistance given in the early stages of crisis. PFA can take anywhere from a few minutes to several hours and has the goal of facilitating coping or problem solving, a breakdown of which is assumed to be the chief characteristic of crisis. Its objectives are: (a) providing support to the caller, (b) taking steps to reduce lethality (e.g., suicide, homicide, and other threats to life and health), and (c) establishing a link to a helping resource to continue assistance in crisis resolution.

Second order crisis intervention, or crisis therapy, refers to short-term counseling which can take anywhere from a few sessions to several months. Its goal is to assist the client in working through the crisis experience (i.e., expressing feelings, achieving cognitive mastery, making behavioral and interpersonal adjustments) toward an ultimate resolution of the crisis.

Second order crisis intervention employs a wide range of therapeutic strategies—based on A. Lazarus' (1976) multimodal behavior therapy—and therefore requires considerably more training than that provided telephone counseling volunteers. The five components of PFA (Slaikeu, in press), however, are, by virtue of their clearly defined objectives (support, reduction of lethality, linkage to helping resources), well suited to telephone counseling work. The five components of PFA are based on a problem-solving model which serves as a "cognitive map" for the telephone counselor to follow in talking to a caller in crisis. The five steps can be summarized as follows:

(a) Making psychological contact is the first component and involves being empathic or "tuning in" to a caller's feelings during a crisis. It means listening to both facts (what happened, who was involved, and the like) and feelings (caller's specific affective reaction to recent events), and reflecting both back during the course of the telephone conversation. Its objective is for the client to feel "heard," understood, and supported during the intense crisis experience.

(b) Exploring dimensions of the problem requires a focus on the immediate past, the present, and the immediate future. In particular, an attempt is made to discover the event(s) that precipitated the current crisis, the effect on the caller and his or her immediate family/social group, and any impending decisions confronting the caller. This second component of PFA includes the assessment of lethality, which provides the data base for subsequent action steps. The objective of this component is to distinguish those aspects of the caller's problem that need immediate attention from those which do not.

(c) Examining possible solutions to the problem involves an assessment of coping strategies, how they have proven ineffective, and what options are available to the caller. An attempt is made to identify possible steps to alleviate the most pressing concerns identified above.

(d) Assisting the caller in taking concrete action means helping him or her take the best next step given the situation. Since the ability of callers to take action steps will vary according to the intensity of the crisis, this requires that telephone counselors make judgments about how directive they should be. Primary considerations, according to this model, are: (a) the degree of lethality, and (b) the ability of the caller to take care of himself or herself at the time of the call. (See Slaikeu, in press, for further detail on the selection of action steps.)

(e) Following up to check progress is the final component of first order crisis intervention. In face-to-face sessions this might be as simple as planning the next appointment, or agreeing for a client to call back in a day or so (after a particular action step has been taken) to report on progress. In telephone counseling this usually means securing at least a first name and phone number to allow for follow-up at a later time. While follow-up is less pressing for some crises, it is critical in others (e.g., suicide and homicide threats, intense personal and social disorganization). The seriousness of many life crises warrant that first order crisis intervention is not complete until some procedure for follow-up has been established.

ONE TOWN'S HOT LINE: BUFFALO, NEW YORK

If you need help for a personal or family problem, call Crisis Services any time of day or night, seven days a week. The number is 834-3131. Crisis Services provides confidential problem-solving by phone; information about 500 helping agencies; direct counseling for personal distress and family discord; assistance for victims of rape and sexual assault, and access to comprehensive mental health and mental retardation services. Workers are on duty 24 hours a day to respond to suicidal calls, crisis situations, and mental health emergencies.

This advertisement, which appears frequently in the *Buffalo Evening News*, sums up succinctly the chief features of Crisis Services, Inc. Originally named the Suicide Prevention and Crisis Service (SPCS) in 1968, the organization was established to meet a need for 24-hour crisis counseling and also to facilitate closer coordination of public and volunteer services in the Buffalo and Erie County area. SPCS in the late 1960s had four telephone lines (advertised separately in the phone book and "personal" columns of the newspaper): Suicide Prevention, Drug Hot Line, Problem of Living Line, and Teen Hot Line, staffed by 80 volunteer telephone counselors.

The volunteers were trained by a professional staff made up of clinical psychologists, social workers, and psychiatric nurses proficient in telephone crisis intervention. An emergency outreach service (crisis intervention in homes, bus depots, and the like) was added in 1973, the year in which SPCS was changed in both name and function. As Crisis Services, Inc. the center shifted from a narrow suicide and crisis focus to a "life stress and crisis counseling" approach (Haywood, 1977). In addition, the center became a central interchange link between citizens and 500 organized human services in the Buffalo area. The life stress and crisis counseling operation is staffed by 150 trained nonpaid telephone counselors who receive training and supervision from a paid professional staff. Through its telephone function, Crisis Services provides the only constant and reliable link between the full range of human services in the Buffalo area. In fact, in the blizzard of 1977, Crisis Services was the only human service that could remain open to help citizens suffering from the psychological stress that accompanied this natural disaster.

The interchange orientation of Crisis Services has a number of other key characteristics:

1) The problem-solving help given to callers in crisis over the telephone takes place in the context of a "stress modulation and health maintenance" framework (Haywood, 1977). The model emphasizes a holistic approach to human functioning, based on clearly articulated human values (e.g., diminishing social alienation and sharing responsibility for problem solving in the community), aimed at building life skills for stress reduction and coping.

2) Crisis Services views its work with callers as both prevention of psychopathology and enhancement of life quality by facilitating growth through resolution of life crises.

3) Innovative services (e.g., a Night People Program for alcoholics, a Care Ring Program for shut-ins, and Hospice Services for the terminally ill) are "spun off" as soon as they are ready to stand on their own. Many of these programs were developed subsequent to assessment of citizens' needs through the center's telephone operation. This approach is consistent with other "clinical-community" strategies where preventive community programs are developed as a direct result of information gleaned from clinical work (see Slaikeu, 1977).

4) Volunteers are still the mainstay of the service, although they are now more appropriately called "nonpaid staff."

5) Every attempt has been made to increase the accessibility of services. For example, anyone in the Buffalo area can pick up a telephone in a police box and be put into direct contact with Crisis Services.

6) Calls are routinely tape recorded for supervision and research purposes.

7) Callers are routinely called back in approximately two weeks for follow-up to check on problem resolution and appropriateness of referral.

EVALUATION OF TELEPHONE CRISIS SERVICES

In the last two decades many articles have been published on the evaluation of telephone counseling services (see Auerbach & Kilmann, 1977; Rosenbaum & Calhoun, 1977). In their detailed analysis of crisis intervention outcome studies, Auerbach and Kilmann (1977) noted that it is virtually impossible to demonstrate a causal relationship between the work of a telephone counseling service and behavior change in an entire community:

> ...variables such as drug usage, divorce rates, and hospitalization rate may be affected by uncontrollable factors such as drug supply, ease of obtaining a divorce based on relaxed laws or easing of social sanctions, and changing criteria for hospital admission, respectively. A more viable general procedure is to demonstrate positive changes in the individuals who have actually utilized the program, and by showing program growth from administrative standpoints (Auerbach & Kilmann, 1977, p. 1198).

Unfortunately, many of the so-called "outcome" studies surveyed by these reviewers had reported only on the outcome of training programs, i.e., the extent to which workers performed on the telephones as they had been trained to do. Few studies had collected data on caller outcome after the call, and even fewer had attempted to establish a link between process and outcome variables.

To date, then, we know very little about the impact, if any, telephone counseling has on callers' resolution of their crises. However, a data base can be established, since, as Auerbach and Kilmann (1977) point out, several studies (e.g., Murphy et al., 1969; Slaikeu et al., 1975; Wilson et al., Note 2) have shown that telephone follow-up of callers is possible. Asking for a first name, a telephone number, and a convenient time to call back enables centers to collect data on how the crisis which led to the initial call is being managed in subsequent days and weeks.

While data for both process and outcome are available (analyses of taped calls and call back of callers), there is still a need for greater precision on what process variables to investigate and what outcome questions to ask. Of the most frequently used process coding systems, Clinical Effectiveness (Knickerbocker & McGee, 1973) continues to present problems in terms of inter-rater reliability, and Technical Effectiveness (Fowler & McGee, 1973), although quite high in reported inter-rater reliability, still captures only a part of what crisis workers are supposed to be offering callers during a crisis call. (See Auerbach & Kilmann, 1977 and Slaikeu et al., 1975, for a more detailed critique of these systems.) The five component model summarized earlier in this chapter—Psychological First-Aid—has the potential to generate a comprehensive, reliable coding system for telephone counseling, although work on developing the coding categories has just begun.

Outcome categories need to be similarly refined. Since crisis is assumed to involve a breakdown in coping mechanisms (Caplan, 1964), follow-up should determine whether there has been any improvement in the caller's ability to cope with the crisis after the telephone contact. According to R. Lazarus' (1980) theoretical framework, this means that follow-up should assess: (a) the caller's ability to manage the "subjective" aspects or feelings associated with the crisis, and (b) the caller's ability to take steps toward solving the immediate problem(s). Studies which have investigated the referral process (France, 1975; Slaikeu et al., 1973, 1975) are examples of follow-up to determine if the "action steps" agreed to in the call were or were not helpful, i.e., one aspect of a caller's problem resolution.

Outcome needs to be considered at (at least) three points: the end of the call, several days after the call, and six weeks or so (Caplan, 1964) following the telephone contact. In the first case, the goal is to determine whether the telephone conversation has been of immediate assistance. In the psychological first aid model presented earlier, this is judged by whether: (a) support has been provided, (b) lethality has been reduced, and (c) linkage to other helping resources has been accomplished. In the second case (a few days later), assessment is made of the caller's coping ability (according to R. Lazarus, 1980, above), checking specifically on action steps agreed to in the initial call. In the third case (several weeks later), crisis theory suggests examination of the nature of the personality reorganization which is taking place (Capan, 1964; Viney, 1976).

A detailed description of research strategies in this framework is beyond the scope of this chapter. (See Slaikeu, in press, for further discussion of these research issues.) For now, however, it can be said that new coding systems need to be developed for process analysis, and that follow-up is both possible and crucial to the development of viable research programs in telephone counseling.

A LOOK TO THE FUTURE

Recent surveys of telephone counseling services (e.g., Motto, 1979; Haywood & Leuthe, Note 1) offer clues to future directions for telephone crisis intervention. In a report on a survey of 50 of the 70 centers holding membership in the International Association for Suicide Prevention, Motto (1979) highlighted changes in both "programs" and "procedures." The chief trend in the former is toward individualized services for such groups as: victims of crime (including rape, battering, sexual abuse), the elderly, grieving families, persons with venereal disease, and single parents. Procedural innovations include technological changes such as the addition of telephone tapes as an adjunct to telephone counseling at the University of Texas at Austin (Iscoe et al., 1979), and a "tele-link" system for group interaction in Brisbane, Australia (Motto, 1979). The main programmatic changes, however, are the addition of activities that go beyond traditional telephone counseling and referral to include outreach services, community education regarding life crises and suicide prevention, and the training of staffs of various community agencies in crisis intervention. In a similar vein, Haywood and Leuthe's (Note 1) survey of 500 centers found that those which had survived the longest were characterized by multiple funding sources, a move toward serving a coordinating function for community services (e.g., The Buffalo Interchange Model), and the development of services designed to meet special community needs.

The most important implication of these findings is that the future of centers rests with their ability to meet the needs both of consumer groups and of other human service agencies in the community. Motto (1979), for example, reports that the Cleveland, Ohio Suicide Prevention Center serves as a 24-hour center for evaluation and referral of psychiatric emergencies for the county emergency medical service, and also handles all emergency telephone calls on nights and weekends for several mental health centers. Similarly, the Montreal Tel-Aide Center is used by Parents Anonymous and other community groups who are then relieved of the burden of having to set up their own 24-hour service.

In the author's view, the way in which hot lines meet the needs of other agencies goes well beyond mere cooperation and instead can be viewed as the formation of a political base which will be necessary to maintain funding in the 1980s. In an era of reduced fedeal spending and bureaucracy, human services will have to rely even more on local and state resources. Iscoe's (1974, 1977) maxim that human services recognize "political realities" suggests that hot lines should work toward making themselves indispensable to other agencies (e.g., handling their nighttime and weekend emergency work, offering 24-hour coverage for "9 to 5" agencies, generating referrals, and the like) in addition to meeting the needs of various consumer constituencies. As funding decisions are made on the local and state level, it will become increasingly important for services such as hot lines to have allies ready to support their budget requests which will be scrutinized all the more carefully in an era of scarce resources.

In addition to these political considerations, it will be necessary for centers to demonstrate an impact on callers' crisis resolution. As suggested earlier in this chapter, many questions remain, although the groundwork for solid outcome research has been laid. The challenge of the next decade will be to conduct studies linking process and outcome (based on caller follow-up) which will refine our understanding of the key ingredients in effective telephone counseling.

Reference Notes

1.   Haywood, C., & Leuthe, J. Crisis intervention in the 1980's: From networking to social influence. Paper presented at the annual meeting of the American Psychological Association, September 4, 1980, Montreal, Canada.

2.   Wilson, K. E., Schaff, J. E., Goke, R., & Harkey, K. B. The relationship between measures of volunteer performance and caller satisfaction: A validation study. In R. K. McGee (Ed.), *An evaluation of the volunteer in suicide prevention*. Final project report. Research grant MH-16861, National Institute of Mental Health, Gainesville, Florida. Center for Crisis Intervention Research, Department of Clinical Psychology, University of Florida, May, 1974.

References

Aguilera, D. C., Messick, J. M., & Farrell, M. S. *Crisis intervention: Theory and methodology.* St. Louis, Mo.: Mosby, 1974.

Auerbach, S., & Kilmann, P. R. Crisis intervention: A review of outcome research. *Psychological Bulletin*, 1977, *84*, 1189-1217.

Baldwin, B. A. Crisis intervention: An overview of theory and practice. *The Counseling Psychologist*, 1979, *8*, 43-52.

Butcher, J. N., & Maudal, G. R. Treatment of the individual in crisis. In I. Weiner (Ed.), *Handbook of clinical methods*. New York: Wiley Interscience, 1976.

Caplan, G. *Principles of preventive psychiatry*. New York: Basic Books, 1964.

Carkhuff, R. R. *Helping in human relations: A primer for lay and professional helpers.* New York: Holt, Rinehart and Winston, Inc., 1969.

France, K. Evaluation of lay volunteer crisis counseling workers. *American Journal of Community Psychology*, 1975, *3*, 197-219.

Fowler, D. E., & McGee, R. K. Assessing the performance of telephone crisis workers: The development of a technical effectiveness scale. In D. Lester & G. Brockopp (Eds.), *Crisis intervention and counseling by telephone*. Springfield, Illinois: Charles C. Thomas, 1973.

Halpern, H. A. Crisis theory: A definitional study. *Community Mental Health Journal*, 1973, *9*, 342-349.

Haywood, C. H. The future role of crisis intervention centers: Theoretical base and principles of intervention. *Crisis Intervention*, 1977, *8*, 56-73.

Iscoe, I. Community psychology and the competent community. *American Psychologist*, 1974, *29*, 607-613.

Iscoe, I. Realities and trade offs in a viable community psychology. *American Journal of Community Psychology*, 1977, *5*, 131-154.

Iscoe, I., Hill, F., Harmon, M., & Coffmann, D. Telephone counseling via cassette tapes. *Journal of Counseling Psychology*, 1979, *26*, 166-168.

Knickerbocker, D. A., & McGee, R. K. Clinical effectiveness of volunteer crisis workers on the telephone. In D. Lester & G. Brockopp (Eds.), *Crisis intervention and counseling by telephone*. Springfield, Illinois: Charles C. Thomas, 1973.

Lazarus, A. *Multimodal behavior therapy*. New York: Springer Publishing Company, 1976.

Lazarus, R. The stress and coping paradigm. In L. A. Bond & J. C. Rosen (Eds.), *Competence and coping during adulthood*. Hanover, N.H.: University Press of New England, 1980.

Lester, D. The use of the telephone in counseling and crisis intervention. In I. D. Pool (Ed.), *The social impact of the telephone*. Boston: MIT Press, 1977.

Lester, D., & Brockopp, G. W. (Eds.), *Crisis intervention and counseling by telephone*. Springfield, Illinois: Charles C. Thomas, 1973.

Levine, M., & Levine, A. *A social history of helping services: Clinic, court, school, and community*. New York: Appleton-Century-Crofts, 1970.

McGee, R. K. *Crisis intervention in the community*. Baltimore: University Park Press, 1974.

Miller, K., & Iscoe, I. The concept of crisis: Current status and mental health implications. *Human Organization*, 1963, *22*, 195-201.

Miller, W. The telephone in out-patient psychotherapy. *American Journal of Psychotherapy*, 1973, *27*, 15-26.

Motto, J. A. New approaches to crisis intervention. *Suicide and Life-Threatening Behavior*, 1979, *9*, 173-184.

Murphy, G. E., Wetzel, R. D., Swallow, C. S., & McClure, J. N. Who calls the suicide prevention center: A study of fifty-five persons calling on their own behalf. *American Journal of Psychiatry*, 1969, *126*, 314-324.

Rosenbaum, A., & Calhoun, J. F. The use of the telephone hotline in crisis intervention: A review. *Journal of Community Psychology*, 1977, *5*, 325-339.

Slaikeu, K. A. The clinical-community approach to community psychology. In B. Wolman (Ed.), *International encyclopedia of psychiatry, psychology, psychoanalysis, & neurology.* Boston: Van Nostrand Reinhold, 1977.

Slaikeu, K. A. *Crisis intervention: A handbook for practice and research.* Boston: Allyn & Bacon, Inc., in press.

Slaikeu, K. A., Lester, D., & Tulkin, S. R. Show vs. no-show: A comparison of referral calls to a suicide prevention and crisis service. *Journal of Consulting and Clinical Psychology,* 1973, *40,* 481-486.

Slaikeu, K. A., Tulkin, S. R., & Speer, D. C. Process and outcome in the evaluation of telephone counseling referrals. *Journal of Consulting and Clinical Psychology,* 1975, *43,* 700-707.

Taplin, V. R. Crisis theory: A critique and reformulation. *Community Mental Health Jounral,* 1971, *17,* 13-23.

Tyhurst, J. S. The role of transition states—including disasters—in mental illness. *Symposium of preventive and social psychiatry.* Walter Reed Army Instiute of Research, 1957, Government Printing Office, Washington, D.C., 1958, 109-373.

Viney, L. L. The concept of crisis: A tool for clinical psychologists. *Bulletin for the British Psychological Society,* 1976, *29,* 387-395.

Walfish, S., Tapp, J. T., Tulkin, S. R., Slaikeu, K. A., & Russell, M. The development of a contract negotiation scale for crisis counseling. *Crisis Intervention,* 1976, *7,* 136-148.

Chapter 6

FAMILY CRISIS INTERVENTION AND THE PREVENTION OF PSYCHIATRIC HOSPITALIZATION

Michael W. Kirby
Paul R. Polak
Theodore C. Weerts

The purpose of this chapter is to outline a community-based program of crisis intervention that serves as an alternative to psychiatric hospitalization. As an introduction, we first describe the southwest Denver catchment area and the comprehensive treatment system in place at Southwest Denver Community Mental Health Services, Inc., a system which has resulted in the use of less than one hospital bed per day for a catchment area of approximately 100,000 persons. Next, we delineate the general conceptual bases underlying this system and the relationship of these conceptualizations to current crisis intervention theory and practice. Finally, we present an overview of the research studies that have evaluated the efficacy of the Southwest Denver system.

SOUTHWEST DENVER COMMUNITY CARE SYSTEM

Description of Catchment Area
and Southwest Denver Community Mental Health Center

The southwest Denver catchment area contains 14 distinctive neighborhoods ranging from designated poverty areas to newer, moderately affluent areas. Most residents are lower-middle class, with intact families. Based on 1970 census data, the following profile emerges: 79% of all households are husband-wife families, with only 10% of all households being single person households; children and adolescents constitute approximately 40% of the total population; ethnically, the percentage of Spanish-surnamed persons has increased dramatically, from 6% of the total population in 1960 to 19% in 1970 and to a projected 33% in 1980. The profile of clients admitted to the Center is highly similar to the foregoing description of the catchment area population.

Southwest Denver CMHC is a non-profit corporation with an annual budget of approximately $1,500,000, the state of Colorado's Division of Mental Health being the largest single source of funds. Five major programs comprise the Center: (a) adult psychiatric services, (b) the Barnum outpost for adult Spanish-surnamed/Chicano clients, (c) the PINE (Persons In New Environments) team, which coordinates treatment of chronically disabled clients and includes a variety of HUD apartments for placement of these clients, (d) children and adolescent services, and (e) the alcohol outpatient program. Approximately 1,200 clients are admitted each year.

Following two years of preliminary work by an active group of community citizens, the Center hired its first director in 1971. Since the mental health center was still in developmental stages, certain philosophical tenets were translated into the structure of the Center from the outset. First, a strong volunteer program was implemented, and the Director of Volunteer Programs was the second employee hired, following only the hiring of the Executive Director. Second, crisis and social systems approaches (Polak, 1968, 1971a, 1971b) were adopted, stressing that staff members should treat the client's immediate social system and not work with the identified client in isolation. Third, in order to facilitate home visits, staff offices were omitted from the design of Center space, although small soundproof cubicles afforded private space for filing, paper work, and telephone calls. Fourth, the personnel system was designed to emphasize work performance rather than professional degrees. Fifth, in the Southwest Denver model, the role of clinicians is similar to that of case managers, as each clinician coordinates all treatment activities for each client under his or her care throughout the client's treatment. Sixth, Southwest Denver CMHC has a board composed of community citizens which exercises direct control over the Center, including responsibility for hiring and firing the Executive Director, setting overall policy, and actively monitoring ongoing programs.

The community-based treatment system in southwest Denver has been described in detail in a number of previously published papers (Polak & Kirby, 1976; Polak, Kirby, & Deitchman, 1979), and, accordingly, will receive only brief discussion here. First, home treatment has been a major priority since the Center's inception. Second, for clients who cannot be treated in their own homes, an inpatient alternative system is available. This system consists of several private homes which contract with the Center to provide food, shelter, and informal care for clients placed in their homes.

Crisis Hostel

The private home system was developed subsequent to experimentation with a crisis hostel (Brook, Kirby, Polak, & Vollman, 1976). The hostel, established at the Fort Logan Mental Health Center in 1970 by the Crisis Intervention Division, was intended to serve as an alternative to inpatient hospitalization. The building was an older home owned by a registered nurse and located in a multiple-unit zoned area of Denver. The hostel provided four beds, with a two-bed apartment serving as a backup. Staff nurses, living within five minutes, were on 24-hour call, in addition to the medical on-call system provided by the crisis unit psychiatrist and Fort Logan's medical staff.

An evaluation of this program was conducted toward the end of the project. This follow-up evaluation of the crisis hostel clients and a control group of hospital patients indicated a trend favoring hospital treatment over the crisis hostel. The major area in which this significant difference occurred was symptom improvement. However, because of staff anxiety concerning the use of phenothiazines in a nonhospital setting, the hospital group received significantly more tranquilization than did the hostel group, and this factor may be responsible for the difference in symptom improvement.

Staff questionnaires completed at the termination of the study pinpointed some of the potential reasons for the lack of success found in this evaluation. While the staff were highly favorable to the concept of an inpatient hostel, the staff also perceived two broad problems with this particular hostel: (a) for acute, short-term admissions, the client stay of a few days was too brief to permit development of a therapeutic setting; the social structure provided by the nurse and her friends was too diffuse to be effective, indicating that a more clearly defined, preexisting structure was required, and(b) at times the hostel was overcrowded, resulting in a less than optimal therapeutic atmosphere.

In conclusion, the theoretical rationale underlying the crisis hostel was inadequately tested by this research because of problems occurring with implementation. Nevertheless, much was learned from this experiment, and the current private home system was a direct outgrowth of the crisis hostel; the private home system capitalized on the strengths of the hostel, yet avoided the hostel's major problems.

Private Home System

This inpatient alternative system was implemented in 1972 with the inception of the mental health center. A total of 15 family sponsors have participated in the program since that time. Currently, the Center contracts with five sponsor families in Southwest Denver, two families (four beds) providing homes for children and three (five beds) for adults. The homes usually function as short-term residential settings for clients undergoing a wide range of crises. For adult clients, approximately 40% of the admissions to the sponsor homes involve clients who are displaying moderate to severe psychotic symptomatology. Approximately ½ of the clients are suffering from severe depression, and 40% to 50% of these clients have entered the home following suicide attempts or extreme suicidal thoughts. While the vast majority of the clients are admitted from the community during periods of crisis, the homes occasionally function as a short term transition setting following psychiatric hospitalization.

In 1979, the adult alternative homes were used for 648 client bed days. During the same period, only ½ as many short-term psychiatric hospital bed days were required for other clients, and this 2:1 ratio has remained stable over the past several years. From the above description of clients in the alternative homes, it is obvious that many more hospital bed days would be required in the absence of our alternative home system.

Admission to the homes is usually arranged during daytime working hours; only 20% of the admissions are performed on an extreme emergency basis during off-hour, on-call periods. Typically, then, clients can be cleared medically and medications can be prescribed by Center staff psychiatrists before the client enters a home. During off-hours, medical clearance and medications are provided when necessary by an on-call physician at a nearby psychiatric hospital.

Upon an admission to a home, the client's therapist provides the family sponsor with a brief description of the events that led up to the admission and details the client's required medications, treatment goals, and restrictions. After admission, staff coverage of the private homes is comprehensive; the homes are well integrated into the Center's overall treatment program and receive considerable support and professional service. Each client is contacted daily by his or her therapist, and a staff psychiatrist and psychiatric nurse evaluate each client's clinical progress at the home at the beginning and end of each work week. In addition, each home is assigned two permanent staff coordinators, and on-call coverage is available for emergencies at all times.

The role that the family sponsors have in the treatment of clients is well circumscribed. The sponsors do not function as therapists. Rather, the home settings intrinsically call into play a complex set of social variables that elicit ''guest'' behavior from clients, rather than symptomatic behavior. The sponsor's role is defined primarily as one of providing a comfortable home setting for the clients. In addition, home sponsors quite naturally become astute observers of client behavior and often provide clinical staff with useful descriptions of their clients' emotional states and thinking processes. However, sponsors are not assigned "observer" responsibilities, and they appear to function better both as caretakers and as observers when their responsibility is limited only to providing a comfortable home.

There are several client characteristics that preclude admission to an alternative home. Clients who are assaultive or extreme suicide risks are generally not admitted to the homes unless staff coverage can be provided continuously. If the assault or suicide risk is seen as being only temporary and if staff time is available, staff coverage will be provided for up to 72 hours, with staff changes being made every three to four hours. Similarly, extremely agitated clients will often not be placed in a home unless staff coverage can be provided during the period of agitation. Clients who are likely to leave without restraint also are not admitted to the homes.

The above exclusions do not represent serious obstacles. Many clients who display assaultive, suicidal, agitated, and runaway behavior in their own home surroundings or in a psychiatric hospital do not display similar behaviors in an alternative home setting. The rule used in the Center is that an alternative home admission is the last alternative to be used, and a hospital admission is even rarer. Hospital admissions for acute treatment are made only when there is extremely good evidence that alternative home treatment has failed or will fail.

Families are used as sponsor home settings because of the preponderance of family units (80% of the residences) in the Southwest Denver catchment area. Over ½ of our severely psychiatrically disabled clients live within family units on a permanent basis, and the sponsor homes are chosen to provide model family units. The sponsor homes naturally provide training in intrafamily communication and appropriate family behavior. Other types of sponsor settings can easily be imagined. Apartment, boarding home, dormitory, and nursing home settings should be equally amenable to a sponsor system, and each should be developed when they represent a likely mode for the long term living arrangements of an area's clients.

CONCEPTUAL BASIS FOR SOUTHWEST DENVER CMHC

The foregoing description of the Center's programs outlined the interrelated techniques of crisis intervention and social systems intervention. The strong emphasis on crisis intervention has been an integral part of the Center's philosophy since its inception. Clients and the members of their immediate social system are viewed as being in a crisis at the point at which the client seeks admission to the Center.

The concept of the "crisis of admission" was developed from research carried out both at Dingleton Hospital in Scotland and later at the Fort Logan Mental Health Center (Polak & Jones, 1973). At the point of admission, prospective clients, members of their families, the referring doctor, and ward staff were asked to discuss, in one another's presence, what they perceived to be the purpose of the client's admission. The results indicated that (a) admission regularly occurred at the height of a social crisis involving the client and his or her primary living group; this event was termed the "crisis of admission", (b) the crisis of admission was the exacerbation of the client's symptoms and usually the final one in a series of social systems crises, each of which was unresolved, and (c) intervention in the social systems crisis which led to admission was as important as the treatment of the client in the hospital.

As with any crisis, this juncture is a critical one in that both the client and his or her immediate social system are at a turning point. If an intervention is effective, the identified client and social system will be strengthened and will have developed new coping techniques; if ineffective, the client may become more dependent upon the treatment system.

From this perspective, it is especially important that, insofar as possible, the client be treated in the community along with members of the immediate social system. An acutely psychotic client who is hospitalized during this crisis may become a chronic mental patient, or one who is dependent on institutions for long periods thereafter (Minkoff, 1978).

If for some reason a client needs to be temporarily separated from the family and community, the private home system offers an effective alternative to the psychiatric hospital. The message conveyed to the client by admission to one of these homes is a positive one, with the family serving as viable role models while encouraging the client to assume responsibility for his or her behavior. Thus, the negative dependency-enhancing effects which accompany institutionalization are circumvented with the private home, and instead the client is placed in a "normal" family setting and is provided considerable support with high expectations for positive behavioral change.

To summarize, the treatment philosophy at Southwest Denver CMHC stresses techniques of crisis intervention and social systems intervention. As the most recent in a series of unresolved crises, the crisis of admission is particularly critical. The client and his or her immediate social system are in crisis, and thus the kind and quality of the intervention have a significant impact on the client's and social system's future level of functioning. Clients are treated in their own homes whenever possible. For clients who need temporary separation from their real-life setting, admission to one of the private homes is the preferred modality; only in rare cases is psychiatric hospitalization appropriate.

RESEARCH AND EVALUATION STUDIES

In 1972, simultaneous with implementation of the inpatient alternative program, a longitudinal study was undertaken to evaluate its effectiveness. At the point of intake and following the decision to admit the client on an inpatient basis, clients were assigned randomly to either a home (experimental group) or the hospital (control group). The same clinical team provided treatment to both the experimental and control groups. All adult clients from the southwest Denver catchment area served as study subjects. No specific criteria were set for the exclusion of certain kinds of clients, such as those too transient, too psychotic, or with a prior history of psychiatric hospitalization. The research design could be broken, however, under special circumstances in which a clinical staff committee felt that it could potentially interfere with optimal treatment.

Data collection occurred at four points: admission, discharge, and at two follow-ups. The first follow-up occurred 4 to 5 months post-discharge, while the second took place 3½ to 4 years post-discharge.

Data were collected from three sources: clinicians, clients, and community informants who typically were close relatives or friends of the client. All information was collected only after the client had received a full description of the study and had voluntarily signed an informed consent form. Four major instruments were employed, with additional instruments added to the second follow-up study. These four instruments were: (a) the Treatment Effectiveness Scale (TES), a client satisfaction measure developed at Fort Logan Mental Health Center and consisting of three subscales—Satisfaction with Self, Satisfaction with Interpersonal Relations, and Satisfaction with Treatment Outcome (Bebeau, 1973), (b) an individualized treatment goal system in which each of the three aforementioned data sources set treatment goals for the client at admission, and subsequently rated perceived degree of attainment at discharge and follow-up, (c) an abbreviated version of Jourard's Self-Disclosure Scale (Jourard, 1971a, 1971b), modified and employed as a measure of family functioning, and (d) a brief measure of community adjustment. All instruments possessed acceptable levels of reliability and internal consistency.

Description of Experimental and Control Groups

A certain percentage of clients randomly assigned to the home group could not actually be treated in the home setting, primarily because they became overtly violent or suicidal and posed management problems. Of the first 48 clients assigned to the original home group, 10 could not be treated in a home. Most of these broken design cases occurred in initial months of the evolution of the home system, and once the system stabilized, the proportion of broken-design cases dropped sharply.

Comparison of selected demographic and psychiatric variables for the original home and hospital groups revealed no apparent differences. When the 10 broken-design cases mentioned above were removed from the original home group, the similarity between the home and hospital groups actually was enhanced, primarily because the vast majority of the broken-design clients were diagnosed "paranoid," and clients with this diagnosis were overrepresented in the original home group.

Discharge Results

Table 1 presents results of selected staff, client, and community informant outcome measures at the point of discharge for the home and hospital groups. As can be seen, there were no differences for any staff measure. However, one significant difference did emerge from the community informant data: a scale measuring satisfaction with treatment outcome (STO) showed a difference in favor of the home group. From the client outcome measures, three significant differences were obtained, involving: again the STO subscale, the entire Treatment Effectiveness Scale, and a measure of perceived staff concern and competence (not shown in Table 1). All three of these differences were in a direction favorable to the home group. In addition to these statistically significant findings, scale means for every client discharge measure favored the home group.

Short-term Follow-up Results

The initial wave of follow-up interviews occurred four months from the point of admission. Each group had about the same average number of days in treatment.

Follow-up interviews were obtained for 32 hospital and 30 home clients, resulting in respective attrition rates of 16% and 19%, which are relatively low rates for this client population.

The outcome results obtained at discharge appeared to maintain at this short-term follow-up (see Table 2). Again, scale means for every measure favored the home group. The one significant group difference found in community informant data at discharge was in the same direction at follow-up, but did not reach significance. Two of the discharge differences indicating greater client satisfaction with treatment outcome and overall treatment effectiveness remained significant in the same direction at follow up.

In addition, two client measures not significantly different at discharge did attain significance at follow-up. First, follow-up ratings of treatment goal attainment (averaged across all goals set at admis-

Table 1
Selected Staff, Client, and Community Informant
Discharge Scores for Home ($N = 37$)
and Hospital ($N = 38$) Groups

Outcome Measures	Home Mean	Hospital Mean	t Value
Total Treatment Effectiveness Scale			
Staff	55.7	54.4	<1
Client	64.0	58.1	2.1*
Community Informant	64.2	58.5	1.9
TES Subscale			
Satisfaction with Treatment Outcome			
Staff	16.6	16.0	<1
Client	19.3	16.5	4.0**- *
Community Informant	20.3	17.3	3.7**- *
Goal Attainment Ratings			
(across all goals set)			
Staff	24.2	23.3	<1
Client	25.3	22.8	1.8
Community Informant	20.5	22.8	<1
Total Self Disclosure to Three Significant Others			
Client	41.6	37.6	<1

* $p < .05$
*** $p < .001$

sion) were significantly higher for clients in the home group. Second, the self-disclosure measure was significantly different, again in favor of the home group.

A series of open-ended questions probed the degree to which ex-clients in both groups identified a specific person as especially important in the treatment process. Responses to these questions were recorded verbatim and subsequently rated by independent judges. The results showed that ex-clients in the home group identified significantly more persons as playing a major role in their treatment. More

Table 2

Selected Client and Community Informant Follow-up
Scores for Home ($N = $ 30)
and Hospital ($N = $ 32) Groups

Outcome Measures	Home Mean	Hospital Mean	t Value
Total Treatment Effectiveness Scale			
Client	61.0	55.3	2.0*
Community Informant	59.7	55.3	1.1
TES Subscale			
Satisfaction with Treatment Outcome			
Client	17.8	15.5	3.0**
Community Informant	18.1	16.7	1.3
Goal Attainment Ratings			
(across all goals set)			
Client	26.9	23.5	2.9**
Community Informant	25.6	23.0	1.6
Total Self-Disclosure to Three Significant Others			
Client	49.9	34.3	2.15*

* $p < .05$
** $p < .01$

over, an analysis of the content of these responses revealed a clearcut tendency for clients in the home group to develop a meaningful relationship with one or more members of the home sponsor family.

Long-term Follow-up Results

When planning began for the second follow-up study, it was decided that two areas of client outcome had been inadequately assessed in previous phases of the research: (a) psychopathology, and (b) psychiatric symptomatology. Accordingly, in addition to the instruments employed in the earlier phases of this longitudinal study, four instruments were added to the interview: (a) the Mini-Mult, a brief form of the MMPI (Kincannon, 1968), (b) the Brief Psychiatric Rating Scale (BPRS), completed by the interviewer as a measure of symptomatology (Overall & Gorham, 1962), (c) a questionnaire which obtained a chronological record of the ex-client's life experiences since the previous follow-up interview, including a complete employment history, all subsequent treatment episodes in either a private or public facility, and dependence on public resources, and (d) a measure consisting of three versions of the Family Environment Scale (FES) (Moos, 1974), which was administered only to ex-clients in the home group; one version focused on the client's own family, another on the client's idealized family, and the third on the client's perception of the home sponsor family in whose home the client had been treated. The results from this assessment of family environment is being prepared for separate publication.

The results reported below are based on interview data collected face-to-face from 27 ex-clients in the home group and 27 ex-clients in the hospital group. Thus, the attrition rates for the home and hospital groups were 30% and 32%, respectively, based on the number of clients in the original intact groups. Attrition rates from first to second follow-up were 13% in the home group and 22% in the hospital group.

The preliminary results of this follow-up study indicate that group differences found at discharge and the first follow-up have dissipated. Indeed, three-and-a-half to four years following discharge, scale means for the two groups do not differ significantly for any measure.

There is a trend, however, for ex-clients in the home group to report a better employment record. More specifically, at the time of the second follow-up interview, 30% of the home group were employed in full-time jobs, in contrast to 19% of the hospital group. Moreover, for those who were employed, the average number of months at their job was 14.0 for the home group, compared to 9.2 for the hospital group.

SUMMARY AND CONCLUSIONS

Southwest Denver Community Mental Health Services, Inc. is a citizen-controlled community mental health center serving the approximately 100,000 persons residing in southwest Denver. Since its inception in 1971, through the use of social systems and crisis intervention techniques, home treatment, and an innovative system of alternatives to hospitalization, Southwest Denver CMHC has reduced the use of hospital beds to less than one bed per day. Social systems treatment emphasizes working with the identified client's immediate social network, usually family members and relatives. Not only are crisis intervention concepts an important and routine part of the treatment process, but the significance of the removal of the client from this system and admission to a psychiatric hospital are clearly recognized. An inpatient alternative system, consisting of private community homes, serves as an alternative to the psychiatric hospital for 85% of all clients needing separation from their families. A longitudinal evaluation of this inpatient alternative system found that clients treated in one of these homes tend to form close personal attachments to the home sponsor family members, and that these clients are significantly more satisfied with the results of their treatment than are clients treated in the psychiatric hospital.

REFERENCES

Bebeau, E. C. Convergent validation of treatment outcome. Unpublished doctoral dissertation, University of Colorado, 1973.

Brook, B. D., Kirby, M. W., Polak, P. R., & Vollman, R. Crisis hostel: An alternative to the acute psychiatric ward. In J. H. Parad, L. H. P. Resnik, & L. G. Parad (Eds.), *Emergency and disaster management: A mental health source book.* Bowie, Maryland: Charles Press, 1976.

Jourard, S. M. *Self-disclosure: An experimental analysis of the transparent self.* New York: John Wiley & Sons, 1971(a).

Jourard, S. M. *The transparent self.* New York: D. Van Nostrand, 1971(b).

Kincannon, J. C. Prediction of the standard MMPI scale scores from 71 items: The Mini-Mult. *Journal of Consulting and Clinical Psychology,* 1968, *3,* 319-325.

Minkoff, K. A map of the chronic patients. In J. A. Talbott (Ed.), *The chronic mental patient.* Washington, D.C.: The American Psychiatric Association, 1978.

Moos, R. The Family Environment Scale Preliminary Manual. Palo Alto, California: Social Ecology Laboratory, Department of Psychiatry, Stanford University, 1974.

Overall, J. E., & Gorham, D. R. The Brief Psychiatric Rating Scale. *Psychological Reports*, 1962, 10, 799-812.

Polak, P. The crisis of admission. *Social Psychiatry*, 1968, *2*(4), 150-158.

Polak, P. The irrelevance of hospital treatment to the patient's social system. *Hospital and Community Psychiatry*, *1971*, *22*(8), 43-44. (a)

Polak, P. Social systems intervention. *Archives of General Psychiatry*, 1971, *25*, 11-117. (b)

Polak, P., & Jones, N. The psychiatric non-hospital: A model for change. *Community Psychiatry*, 1973, *9*, 2.

Polak, P., & Kirby, M. W. A model to replace psychiatric hospitals. *The Journal of Nervous and Mental Disease*, 1976, *162*(1), 13-22.

Polak, P., Kirby, M. W., & Deitchman, W. Treating acutely psychotic patients in private homes. *New Directions for Mental Health Services*, 1979, *1*, 49-64.

Chapter 7

CRISIS INTERVENTION FOR MEDICAL PROBLEMS

Rita Yopp Cohen

Crisis intervention has continued to grow in prominence in recent years and now seems firmly entrenched as one treatment method for dealing with basically healthy individuals who are attempting to resolve problems arising from a known precipitant. Yet the systematic application of crisis theory and crisis management techniques to problems with precipitants of a medical nature whose resolution involves psychological adjustment has been lacking. While occasional references to the use of crisis intervention with medical patients are noted (Leitner, 1974), there appears to be no systematic adaptation of the theory and techniques for medical patients.

The purpose of this chapter is to suggest that the health care needs of individuals in the United States are changing rapidly, that the health care system has not yet adequately addressed those needs, and that a systematic application of crisis theory and techniques to individuals with health care problems may represent a useful means of delivering services. The first section of the chapter will document the changing health care needs of individuals due to changing patterns of illness and alterations within the health care system. The next section will delineate the ways in which certain medical problems do and do not fit a crisis theory model, while the third section will survey the existing programs and their evaluation; although many of the current

127

programs utilize components of a crisis model, they have not necessarily identified themselves as crisis intervention programs. In addition, there are several programs that do not utilize crisis techniques or theory; however, the positive results of such programs may be achievable by utilizing crisis techniques, which are likely to be less costly and potentially more efficient than other methods of delivery such as group psychotherapy.

CHANGING HEALTH CARE PATTERNS
WITHIN THE UNITED STATES

Since the turn of the century, mortality from acute illness has decreased dramatically in the United States. During the first half of the century, control, prevention, or cure of infectious diseases such as influenza and tuberculosis proceeded at a rapid pace. By 1955, 81.4% of all deaths were attributable to chronic illnesses, not infectious diseases. In 1900, pneumonia, tuberculosis, gastritis, and influenza accounted for 35% of all deaths; by 1960, neoplasms, cardiovascular disease, and vascular lesions of the central nervous system accounted for 65.6% of deaths (Bright, 1966).

Accompanying the changing patterns of illness is an increase in the life expectancy of the population and concomitantly, an increase in the number of individuals with chronic disease. Currently, chronic illnesses account for 70% of all visits to a physician (Gerson & Strauss, 1975). Thus, the challenges facing the health care delivery system now differ from those of even the earlier part of the century.

Since the characteristics of chronic disease differ from those of acute illness, the goals and methods of treatment must also differ. Chronic diseases are, by definition, incurable; so the goal of treatment is not a return to previous health, but the monitoring and control of the progression of disease and prevention of further deterioration. Typically, a degree of physical and psychological adjustment is necessary for an individual to manage his or her illness effectively. For example, most patients with multiple sclerosis will have some physical difficulty. Patients may also have difficulty accepting the unpredictable and uncontrollable course of the disease. If a patient limits his or her activity due to fear of the disease, the effects of illness are not simply physical, but emotional and social as well. Additionally, many chronically ill individuals are expected to function as healthy people, yet their daily routine may require substantial alterations to maintain adequate disease control. For example, a diabetic may require restricted diets, regular mealtimes, or insulin injections, yet be expected to maintain the same lifestyle as an unimpaired individual. Obviously, the management of chronic diseases such as diabetes usually requires far more patient participation than acute illnesses. For acute illness, almost all care is provided by medical personnel. However, for many chronic diseases, after initial diagnosis there is little need for direct medical intervention, except for routine monitoring and during medical emergencies. Therefore, much of the assistance a chronically ill individual requires is more likely to be social and behavioral rather than medical. Patients may need assistance in implementing behavior change, adjusting to the consequences of having a lifelong illness, or simply obtaining adequate information on available facilities and resources.

Another important change has occurred within the health care system in conjunction with the increasing numbers of chronically ill individuals; consumers and medical personnel are becoming more aware of the importance of the total patient including physical, psychological, and social status. The changing focus is reflected not only in chronic disease management but in curative medicine as a preference for conservative rather than radical procedures as the initial treatment of choice. For example, a radical mastectomy is no longer the only recognized treatment for breast cancer. Researchers are asking whether one can achieve a comparable reduction in death rates from breast cancer through the use of less disfiguring operations; also, the number of hysterectomies performed has been radically reduced in recent years as philosophy changes from emphasizing surgery at the first stage of abnormality to more careful patient monitoring. In other words, a more humanistic emphasis is evolving. With the changing emphasis, the psychosocial needs of patients are becoming more salient.

The consumer movement has been instrumental in achieving recognition by medical personnel of the importance of nonmedical factors in patient care. Consumers are demanding more information to enable them to participate in their own care and to utilize medical resources more efficiently. The astronomical growth of self help groups in recent years attests to the fact that people perceive a need for assistance that the medical care system is not providing. It is likely that the desire for assistance in meeting one's psychological as well as physical needs is a major factor accounting for the proliferation of such groups (Katz & Bender, 1976).

Finally, the consumer movement has also affected the economics of the health care system. By participating more in one's own health management, one develops a better understanding of how the health care delivery system functions and what questions need to be asked. In an age of accountability, the effort to promote cost containment may take the form of utilizing alternative delivery systems such as self help groups, paraprofessionals or expanded function auxiliary personnel, or demanding better patient education to provide the individual with the management tools necessary for disease control.

While all of the aforementioned changes in health care needs, delivery systems, and therapeutic goals are of interest to psychologists as well as other caregiving professionals, one aspect of health care that is central to the interests of psychologists is the relationship between psychological factors and physical illness. There are several hypothesized relationships between psychological and physical health. First, psychological factors may have some role in the etiology of medical illness; psychological stress may alter one's physiological responses and subsequently adversely affect health. For example, Cobb and Rose (1973) studied air traffic controllers who are presumably under chronic stress, and found a higher incidence of hypertension, peptic ulcer, and diabetes in controllers compared to those in similar jobs. Second, psychological problems may exacerbate an illness by interfering with a patient's ability or desire to perform requisite behaviors to control the illness. For example, hypertension can be controlled by taking medication. However, if one cannot acknowledge that one has a chronic illness, one may not take medication. In this case, a disease which can easily be controlled is not managed effectively because the patient is psychologically "unable" to manage the illness. A third way that psychological and medical problems are related is if medical difficulties produce or exacerbate psychological distress; a medical problem may affect one's coping abilities by producing psychological dysfunction such as confusion or increased irritability. In addition, the medical problem may result in disability due to the social stigma attached to an ill or disabled individual. For example, most epileptics are able to control their symptoms with medication, but the stigma and stereotypes attached to epilepsy may make it difficult for one to function "normally." In such cases, an illness which has essentially been medically controlled results in what may become a permanent change in psychological health status. Clearly, psychological factors are of importance when a medical illness is present. The next section will delineate the ways in which crisis theory and crisis intervention techniques might be useful in developing strategies for meeting the psychosocial needs of medical patients.

APPLICATION OF CRISIS THEORY
TO HEALTH CARE PROBLEMS

Although there is no single theory of crisis intervention, one can identify several characteristics of the approach which are consistently cited by those working within the field. While some of the characteristics of crises, premises of crisis theory, and crisis intervention techniques do not directly apply to medical problems, most components of current theory may reasonably be applied to health problems.

First, most crisis theorists suggest that there is a specific, identifiable precipitant of the crisis; it may be loss of a job, the breakup of a relationship, etc. and one of the first steps in crisis intervention is the identification of the event (Bloom, 1963). For medical problems, the external precipitant (i.e., the illness) is quite apparent. In cases where illness onset is sudden such as injury or stroke, the physical event clearly marks the beginning of the crisis episode. For illnesses which require diagnosis to determine that there is illness present and whose onset may be insidious, the crisis may begin long before the medical determination of a problem is made. For instance, in the case of diabetes, an individual may experience symptoms such as excessive thirst, may have had a relative with diabetes, and may suspect that he or she is diabetic. The concern, fear of the disease, etc., could precipitate a crisis and actual diagnosis may merely confirm one's suspicions. In this case, diagnosis may be one phase in the crisis or it may represent a temporary resolution, if the diagnosis is negative. Therefore, while diagnosis is often the precipitant of a crisis, it is not necessarily the first precipitant in a medical crisis episode nor the final resolution of the problem.

A second component of crisis theory which is applicable to medical problems is that patients experience a great deal of subjective distress. A clear precipitant is a necessary although not sufficient condition for a crisis state. Some individuals may react to the diagnosis of medical problems with relatively little distress, particularly if the illness is not highly symptomatic or debilitating. However, those illnesses which require a major alteration of lifestyle and which do not afford the incentive of a return to a high level of wellness if one adheres to medical recommendations are likely to produce a great deal of subjective distress. Physical disability, such as that produced by amputation, or lifestyle disruption, such as that produced by kidney dialysis, exemplify those illnesses which are likely to produce a high level of distress.

The high level of distress is probably, in part, attributable to the third characteristic of crisis situations, namely, that the situation is novel and one's usual coping mechanisms may be inadequate or inappropriate. For example, if one's usual coping style is to ignore problems, it is likely to be difficult coping with confinement to a wheelchair, hospitalization for a myocardial infarction, or required dietary modification to control illness. One's coping skills may be inadequate because of the novelty of the situation or because of the stage in life at which the illness occurs. For example, in most cases, it is likely that adults have a greater repertoire of coping responses due to a greater range of experience than do children or adolescents (Moos & Tsu, 1977). In addition, the psychological meaning of illness may vary depending on age. A hysterectomy may be more psychologically traumatic to a woman in her 20s than a woman in her 50s who has already had children.

Still a fourth assumption of crisis theory is that one is dealing with normal individuals in abnormal situations. One may encounter some individuals who have had chronic psychological difficulties but the assumption is made that, in most cases, the individuals involved were reasonably well adjusted before the medical emergency and will be relatively well adjsuted once they are provided with assistance in developing whatever skills and resources are necessary to adapt to the novel situation. The problem which they face may be different from those faced prior to illness, but it is assumed that most people are capable of developing requisite skills and achieving psychological adaptation.

A related assumption of crisis theory is that those who provide assistance intervene at the stage of crisis to prevent major problems which might develop in the future if the crisis is not resolved successfully. In the case of medical crises, an intervention may consist of educational efforts to teach new ways of performing behaviors as in physical rehabilitation, providing support such as one might provide to a mastectomy patient to enhance her self image and restore marital harmony, teaching methods of altering life style patterns as is required in the management of diabetes, or providing information about a disease so that one might develop reasonable expectations in the case of a disease such as multiple sclerosis where one's own actions have little effect on the medical progression of the disease. Initially the crisis intervener, whether a medical or lay provider, assumes a very active role since a corollary to the assumption that one intervenes to prevent future difficulties is the assumption that one is intervening at a time when individuals feel powerless to cope with a problem and are thus more susceptible to the influence of others. Patients experience a crisis because they lack requisite coping skills; therefore, the crisis worker is often very directive so that a patient may have the time and assistance needed to acquire coping skills.

The types of interventions just cited illustrate still another assumption of crisis theory which is applicable in medical cases, namely, that two major functions of the intervention are to provide information and social support. In one of the background papers written for the Surgeon General's report on health promotion and disease prevention, Hamburg and Killilea (1979) cite three coping strategies for dealing with the stress produced by physical illness: (a) cognitive strategies such as providing information, (b) affective strategies such as providing emotional support, and (c) instrumental strategies such as teaching tangible skills for managing concrete difficulties. While crisis theory has traditionally relied heavily upon providing information and support, providing solutions to behavioral management difficulties by helping the individual to acquire skills such as preparing meals has not been a major focus of crisis intervention. It is likely that the teaching of instrumental responses would become important in medical crisis intervention, where some problems may center around overcoming daily barriers to routine functioning.

A final characteristic of traditional crisis intervention is the reliance on paraprofessional service providers. Since one is dealing with well adjusted individuals who need informaion and support to cope with a novel situation, it is assumed that patients need not necessarily receive assistance from professional providers. The *helper therapy* principle is appropriate for many medical crises as is evident from the proliferation of self help recovery groups. Such groups will be described in more detail in a later section of the chapter but it is important to note that assistance from one who has experienced the same illness is an important part of both the self help group and of many programs begun under the auspices of medical facilities to assist patients in coping with their medical difficulties.

CHARACTERISTICS OF HEALTH CARE PROBLEMS THAT DIFFER FROM A CRISIS MODEL OF INTERVENTION

As is evident from the previous section, there are many commonalities between the treatment of psychological problems via a crisis approach and the treatment of psychological problems related to physical health status. However, medical and psychological crises differ on important characteristics. The impact such differences will have on treatment methods remains to be investigated but it is logical that there will have to be some variations in treatment.

The most important difference between most medical and psychological crises is that many of the medical problems are not time limited events. With the exception of recovery from illnesses where the individual will eventually return to a previous level of functioning, many of the medical problems requiring psychological adaptation are not discrete events; chronic diseases, some types of surgery such as colostomy, or physical handicaps are permanent changes for the patient. Rather than one episode of illness there is a series of continually changing events. For example, a diabetic may be newly diagnosed; the diagnosis represents a discrete event which may precipitate a crisis. In addition, the patient may experience a crisis after having attended patient education groups when the full impact of the medical problem is realized. The patient may also experience crisis the first time that the illness interferes with or prevents the individual from carrying out a normal activity, when a complication such as blindness or kidney failure develops, or when a friend or relative with the same illness experiences severe problems or develops complications. Each individual episode of illness may be viewed as a discrete event, but it would be less than optimal care if the crisis intervener merely reacted to each event without an understanding of previous events or anticipation of possible future crisis precipitants.

Much of the difference between medical and psychological crises may be semantic. While one may define an event such as divorce as a discrete event for which a time limited crisis may follow, clearly, there may be future results of divorce which may create crisis situations; for example, it may be necessary to find a job after having been at home for years, or one may be separated from children. Medical cases differ in that the original precipitating events are in most cases present throughout one's life. Although one must continually cope with the consequences of divorce, the proceedings may occur and pass; but a physical illness such as multiple sclerosis, diabetes, or handicap following injury is always present in the form of concrete, daily reminders of illness, such as required medication, dietary routines, or difficulties in performing certain tasks.

Another way in which crisis situations arising from medical problems differ from others is that some medical conditions may produce or exaggerate psychological symptoms. A good example is the confusion which many patients experience following open heart surgery. While a clear dichotomy between psychological symptoms of a medical versus psychological origin would be artificial, it is important to differentiate those cases where symptoms represent a real lack of coping mechanisms and those where symptoms may be more physiological. Those symptoms related to the medical problem may simply require a factual explanation to the patient, and one wants to alleviate a crisis with as little intervention as possible since one of the effects of illness may already be to decrease an individual's feeling of self control (Haan, 1979). If, however, symptoms represent a lack of coping skills, further assistance and information will be required.

SURVEY OF CURRENT PROGRAMS

Having delineated the ways in which medical problems do or do not fit a crisis model, it is important to survey the programs currently available to patients which utilize some components of a crisis model or illustrate the importance of addressing the psychosocial needs of patients but are not actually crisis intervention programs. Such programs may be classified as proactive or reactive interventions, the former occurring prior to the actual medical emergency and the latter occurring after a medical problem has developed. Proactive medical crisis interventions are similar to those community mental health programs which attempt to anticipate and prevent a crisis by intervening before a stressful event occurs, while reactive interventions are similar to "traditional" crisis interventions, occurring after the crisis precipitant.

There are currently two main types of proactive programs, namely those that prepare patients for surgery and those that undertake preventive health intervention in a nonmedically ill "at-risk" population. Extensive reviews of the literature are available concerning the research on psychological preparation for surgery (Auerbach & Kilmann, 1977; Olbrisch, 1977; Reading, 1979). In most cases, patients receive information and/or supportive interventions prior to surgery. Those individuals are generally compared to a group of patients who either received no intervention or interventions of a different nature. The outcome variables are usually physical, such as amount of pain medication required, length of hospitalization, or number of complications, and, at times, psychological, and are usually confined to the period immediately following surgery until the time of release from the hospital. Few long-term follow-ups of patients after release from the hospital have been attempted.

One example of a presurgical intervention is a study by Langer, Janis, and Wolfer (1975). Patients about to undergo major surgery were provided with either information and encouragement or techniques of cognitive reappraisal of the anxiety provoking aspects of surgery. Those patients who were taught cognitive reappraisal required significantly fewer analgesics than those provided only with information. In a second study (Davis, 1974), one of the few in which the intervention was identified as crisis intervention, patients in the experimental group received a visit by a counselor prior to surgery. Those patients receiving the intervention had a shorter period of hospitalization than those in no treatment or attention-placebo control groups. In general, patients receiving interventions prior to surgery recover with fewer complications or in a shorter time than those patients receiving no intervention or minimal attention-placebo interventions; unfortunately, many of the studies suffer from methodological flaws, primarily due to select patient samples, nonequivalent methods of assigning patients to treatment groups, or lack of appropriate control groups (Auerbach & Kilmann, 1977; Olbrisch, 1977). However, in spite of methodological flaws, the general convergence of positive findings from many studies with differing methodological weaknesses suggests that such interventions do have a positive impact on patient recovery.

A second type of proactive intervention attempts to alter the behavior of individuals who are not currently medically ill but who are "at-risk" for illness. For example, the Multiple Risk Factor Intervention Trial (MR FIT) program is a national clinical trial in which men who are considered to be a high risk for a heart attack because of high blood pressure, cigarette smoking, and high cholesterol are identified and enrolled in a program to reduce the risk factors (National Heart and Lung Insitute, 1976). The program is a five-year prospective study designed to ascertain whether risk factor reduction can reduce the likelihood of a heart attack. Patients are told that they are "at risk" and, more importantly, are taught that the reduction of risk factors is under their control, although it remains to be seen whether they can concomitantly reduce the likelihood of a heart attack by reducing the risk factors. Such a clinical trial presents a unique and interesting example of crisis intervention because one is identifying clinically "healthy" individuals and creating a medical crisis in that one is, in a sense, convincing individuals who feel well that their health is not normal. While the program is currently assessing the effects of a change in health habits on the incidence of heart attack, there is no attempt to assess the psychological impact of the intervention or to view the program as an attempt to resolve a crisis, albeit experimentally induced, via information and social support. Yet information and social support are the two primary mechanisms used in the program. Group sessions of patients and their spouses are conducted in which education and peer support are utilized to promote behavior change. It would be interesting to investigate those patients who either fail to respond to treatment or who decline to participate in the program after screening since presumably some may have experienced a crisis at the time of "diagnosis" as "high-risk" for a heart attack. While the MR FIT program is one of the largest prevention efforts, other interventions such as obesity reduction or smoking cessation groups which focus on the medical advantages of behavior change create similar environments, although patients identify themselves as "at-risk" and presumably come to the programs with somewhat different motives than do MR FIT patients.

The second type of program currently available, namely reactive interventions, is more similar to the problems and techniques usually identified as crisis intervention than are the proactive groups. There are two main categories of reactive interventions, short-term counseling groups for medical patients and self help groups.

Counseling groups may be used for newly diagnosed patients, for rehabilitation of patients, and for behavior change enhancement for those medical conditions requiring active self monitoring. They are more similar to crisis intervention than to traditional psychotherapy groups in that patients are responding to a discrete precipitant, are psychologically normal individuals, and the interventions are often time limited and generally provide information and social support. A good example of the format of counseling groups for newly diagnosed patients is groups conducted for multiple sclerosis patients (Hartings, Pavlou, & Davis, 1976). Groups consisting of approximately 10 patients and spouses are conducted by a psychologist for approximately 10 weeks. The groups attempt to provide information on the medical management, likely problems and their potential impact on family and on vocation, likely adjustment problems to physical disability stemming from MS, and to share experiences and reactions with other patients. The patients are not placed in groups with the assumption that they need psychotherapy; rather it is assumed that every patient may need information and support in adjusting to the illness. Such groups may be run for many illnesses including cancer, kidney failure, etc. (Buchanan, 1975; Hesse, 1975; Huberty, 1974; Kleiman, Mantell, & Alexander, 1977). The particular emphasis of a group may be more on information or support and may vary depending on whether a patient may exercise some control over the course of the disease or requires adaptation to a condition over which he or she has little control.

A second type of counseling group is organized for rehabilitation of patients for whom some recovery may be expected or who will need to adjust to vast difficulties in mobility. Stroke victims, coronary patients, or victims of accidents or illness requiring major physical disability such as amputation are among the patient populations for which groups are found (Rahe, O'Neil, Hagan & Arthur, 1975; Rogers, MacBride, Whylie, & Freeman, 1977). These groups differ mainly in emphasis from the groups for newly diagnosed patients. In addition to information and social support, a major function of such groups is to assist individuals in managing concrete daily tasks.

Finally, counseling groups to accomplish behavior change are conducted for those illnesses whose progress may be substantially affected by the patient's behavior. The techniques are similar to those used in preventive behavior change groups; however, these groups are conducted after an illness is diagnosed. Examples of diseases for which such groups are appropriate include diabetes and hypertension, and may be referred to as patient education groups although even in the context of education, patients may provide mutual social support (Cohen, 1977).

Most reports in the literature of counseling groups, with the exception of behavior change groups, are merely program descriptions. There is inadequate evaluation of the impact of the groups if any evaluation is conducted. Often the outcome measures consist of patient satisfaction or the amount of factual knowledge acquired. The full psychological impact of the groups remains unassessed with a few exceptions (Ibrahim, Feldman, Sultz, Staiman, Young, & Dean, 1974; Rahe et al., 1975). Thus, the establishment of short-term groups for medical problems remains a widely described and intuitively valid approach to treatment, but more rigorous research is needed. Two fairly well controlled studies which investigated the impact of counseling groups on recovery yielded positive results. One study which investigated the effect of group psychotherapy on patients recovering from myocardial infarctions found that the one year survival rate of patients in the experimental group was 10% higher than that in the control group; in addition, of those patients rehospitalized during the year, the average stay of those in the experimental group was 10 days shorter than that in the control group (Ibrahim et al., 1974). A second study in which myocardial infarction patients in the treatment group received ½ hour a day counseling until their release demonstrated a shorter hospitalization and fewer days spent in the coronary intensive care unit for treatment compared to control patients (Gruen, 1975). While psychotherapy groups are not crisis interventions, the positive results demonstrate the effect of psychological factors on recovery. It is possible that groups which utilize crisis techniques may be just as effective as psychotherapeutic groups.

The final type of reactive program to be described is the self help group. Many of the services delivered are analogous to those of the counseling groups, but the groups are conducted by the patients themselves (i.e., paraprofessionals or nonprofessionals). Particularly prolific are the self help groups which address themselves to health related behaviors and chronic health problems (Gartner & Riessman, 1977). They stress the involvement of patients as active participants in their own health, the mutual support provided by others responding to the same event, and problem solving through active coping (Gartner & Riessman, 1977; Gussow, 1976). The illnesses that self help groups address as well as the techniques they utilize are similar to those groups conducted within the health care system and include problems such as adaptation to diabetes, arthritis, asthma, cystic fibrosis, epilepsy, cancer, and amputation. The function of the groups could be to assist patients with a medical problem in adjusting to the illness, as is the case for cancer or mastectomy patients, or they may engage in activities aimed at behavior change, as is the case for obesity groups. Unfortunately, with the exception of those groups centering around mental health and some of the weight reduction groups, very few methodologically sound evaluations of the groups have been conducted (Jordan & Levitz, 1973; Levy, 1978). However, the rapid growth in membership in such organizations suggests that a need is being addressed that the traditional caregiving systems have failed to satisfy. Although the membership is self selected and many groups do not keep adequate records (Levy, 1978), self help groups seem a fruitful area for research investigating the effectiveness of information and mutual support within a crisis theory framework.

SUMMARY

It is useful to identify the commonalities among the programs mentioned, if one is to begin to examine health care problems from a crisis theory orientation. With varying degrees of emphasis, all attempt to deal with the affective, cognitive, and instrumental aspects of coping (Hamburg & Killelea, 1979). Some may rely mainly on cognitive (information) strategies as in surgical preparation, others on instrumental learning and supportive strategies as for stroke victims, but it is difficult to imagine a medical situation where all three need not be addressed to some degree.

Secondly, in teaching active coping, all programs are founded on the assumption that the most effective adaptation is accomplished by providing the patient with a variety of response strategies. Peers may suggest means of coping and it seems likely that one of the contributions of groups to the patient is the opportunity to observe different means by which individuals cope with the same problem.

Lastly, even the professionally organized groups rely heavily on the support and role models of peers. Only the presurgical interventions do not utilize others who have experienced the same illness as change agents in the intervention. Thus, it seems that paraprofessionals and nonprofessionals are viewed not only as cost efficient, but possibly as the most effective providers of care.

EVALUATION OF PRESENT PROGRAMS
AND RECOMMENDATIONS FOR FUTURE DEVELOPMENT

Perhaps the greatest need in evaluating the effectiveness of crisis intervention for medical problems is the recognition by researchers and those working with patients that much of their activity can be theoretically identified as crisis intervention. Currently, no systematic testing of hypotheses arising from a crisis intervention approach to medical problems exists. The thousands of programs in existence testify to the need for some intervention aimed at assisting patients and families in coping with the adjustment problems of medical illness. However, most programs arise in isolation and are loosely based on the assumption that some form of group intervention is the most appropriate strategy. Without identifying a theoretical framework, it is difficult to systematically evaluate a program and, in particular, to evaluate the necessity and effectiveness of various components of a program, since one lacks a solid basis for formulating hypotheses.

Not only is there no theoretical framework guiding much of the research but many of the programs lack any methodologically sound evaluation. Much of the literature involves merely a global description of patient groups. Treatment is not described in enough detail to be replicated or systematically evaluated. There are often so many different treatments occurring within the same program that one has difficulty attributing results to any particular intervention strategy, and there is often no control group or baseline data.

Those studies that do attempt to evaluate treatment in a methodologically sound manner often confine themselves to outcome measures of physical status. Physical measures are clearly necessary but quite insufficient if one is attempting to document the impact of an intervention on the whole person; social status indicators, perceived well-being, and familial adjustment are all important. A social-psychological viewpoint is necessary in addition to a medical perspective.

Finally, if adequate social psychological evaluation is to be conducted, measures of long-term adjustment are necessary. Since the full impact of an illness may not be felt for several years after diagnosis, longitudinal research is clearly indicated. Within a crisis intervention framework, such research could prove a useful test of assumptions made by crisis intervention theorists. As an example, one could examine whether immediate, brief interventions do in fact reduce the number or severity of future difficulties.

It seems likely that once adequate evaluations are conducted, researchers will be faced with a new set of problems similar to those being addressed by researchers investigating the effectiveness of psychotherapy, namely, that the assumption of homogeneity of populations is a simplistic one when dealing with psychological adjustment to various medical problems. What seems to be indicated is research which evaluates the effectiveness of specific interventions with specific types of patients for specific illnesses. There are likely to be some approaches that are generalizable to many problems, but some approaches must surely be more effective with particular illnesses (Cohen & Lazarus, 1979). In addition, various coping strategies may be more or less useful at different stages of an illness. For example, passivity would be quite appropriate immediately following a myocardial infarction but may be detrimental to recovery in the months following release from the hospital. Thus, researchers need more information concerning the psychological impact and useful coping strategies at various stages of an illness.

In summary, one can theoretically identify crisis techniques as being appropriate for medical problems and one can identify many programs designed to deal with the psychological impact of an illness and to provide patients with necessary coping skills. What remains to be accomplished is the integration of the two into a systematic program of research and treatment whose effectiveness is demonstrated using appropriate outcome measures within a sound methodological framework.

REFERENCES

Auerbach, S. M., & Kilmann, P. R. Crisis intervention: A review of outcome research. *Psychological Bulletin,* 1977, *84*(6), 1189-1217.

Bloom, B. L. Definitional aspects of the crisis concept. *Journal of Consulting and Clinical Psychology,* 1963, *27,* 498-503.

Bright, M. Demographic background for programming for chronic diseases in the United States. In A. M. Lilienfeld & A. J. Gifford (Eds.), *Chronic diseases and public health.* Baltimore: The Johns Hopkins Press, 1966.

Buchanan, D. C. Group therapy for kidney transplant patients. *International Journal of Psychiatry in Medicine,* 1975, *6*(4), 523-531.

Cobb, S., & Rose, R. M. Hypertension, peptic ulcer, and diabetes in air traffic controllers. *Journal of the American Medical Association,* 1973, *224,* 489-492.

Cohen, F., & Lazarus, R. S. Coping with the stresses of illness. In G. S. Stone et al. (Eds.), *Health psychology.* San Francisco: Jossey Bass, 1979.

Cohen, R. Y. The development of a group education and management program for low income diabetic and hypertensive patients (Doctoral dissertation, Florida State University, 1977). *Dissertation Abstracts International*, 1978, *38*, 3869B. (University Microfilms No. 7731026).

Davis, H. S. The role of crisis intervention treatment in the patient's recovery from elective surgery (Doctoral dissertation, Northwestern University, 1973). *Dissertation Abstracts International*, 1974, *34*, 3490B. (University Microfilms No. 73-30, 570).

Gartner, A., & Riessman, F. *Self-help in the human services*. San Francisco: Jossey-Bass, Inc., 1977.

Gerson, E. M., & Strauss, A. L. Time for living: Problems in chronic illness care. *Social Policy*, 1975, *6*, 12-18.

Gruen, W. Effects of brief psychotherapy during the hospitalization period on the recovery process in heart attacks. *Journal of Consulting and Clinical Psychology*, 1975, *43*, 223-232.

Gussow, Z. The role of self-help clubs in adaptation to chronic illness and disability. *Social Science and Medicine*, 1976, *10*, 407-414.

Haan, N. G. Psychosocial meanings of unfavorable medical forecasts. In G. S. Stone et al. (Eds.), *Health Psychology*. San Francisco: Jossey Bass, 1979.

Hamburg, B. A., & Killilea, M. Relation of social support, stress, illness, and use of health services. In U.S. Department of Health, Education, and Welfare, *Healthy people: The surgeon general's report on health promotion and disease prevention background papers*. Washington: U.S. Government Printing Office, 1979.

Hartings, M. F., Pavlou, M. M., & Davis, F. A. Group counseling of MS patients in a program of comprehensive care. *Journal of Chronic Disease*, 1976, *29*, 65-73.

Hesse, K. A. Meeting the psychosocial needs of pacemaker patients. *International Journal of Psychiatry in Medicine*, 1975, *6*(3), 359-372.

Huberty, D. J. Adapting to illness through family groups. *International Journal of Psychiatry in Medicine*, 1974, *5*(3), 231-242.

Ibrahim, M. A., Feldman, J. G., Sultz, H. A., Staiman, M. G., Young, L. J., & Dean, D. Management after myocardial infarction: A controlled trial of the effect of group psychotherapy. *International Journal of Psychiatry in Medicine*, 1974, *5*(3), 253-268.

Jordan, H. A., & Levitz, L. S. Behavior modification in a self-help group. *Journal of the American Dietetic Association*, 1973, *62*, 27-29.

Katz, A. H., & Bender, E. I. (Eds.). *The strength in us*. New York: New Viewpoints, 1976.

Kleiman, M. A., Mantell, J. E., & Alexander, E. S. Rx for social death: The cancer patient as counselor. *Community Mental Health Journal*, 1977, *13*, 115-124.

Langer, E. J., Janis, I. L., & Wolfer, J. A. Reduction of psychological stress in surgical patients. *Journal of Experimental Social Psychology*, 1975, *11*, 155-165.

Leitner, L. A. Crisis counseling may save a life. *Journal of Rehabiitation*, 1974, *40*(4), 19-20.

Levy, L. H. Self-help groups viewed by mental health professionals: A survey and comments. *American Journal of Community Psychology*, 1978, *6*, 305-313.

Moos, R. H., & Tsu, V. D. The crisis of physical illness: An overview. In R. H. Moos (Ed.), *Coping with physical illness*. New York: Plenum, 1977.

National Heart and Lung Institute. The multiple risk factor intervention trial (MR FIT). *Journal of the American Medical Association*, 1976, *235*, 825-827.

Olbrisch, M. E. Psychotherapeutic interventions in physical health. *American Psychologist*, 1977, *32*, 761-777.

Rahe, R. H., O'Neil, T., Hagan, A., & Arthur, R. J. Brief group therapy following myocardial infarction: Eighteen month followup of a controlled trial. *International Journal of Psychiatry in Medicine*, 1975, *6*(3), 349-358.

Reading, A. E. The short term effects of psychological preparation for surgery. *Social Science and Medicine*, 1979, *13A*, 641-654.

Rogers, J., MacBride, A., Whylie, B., & Freeman, S. J. The use of groups in the rehabilitation of amputees. *International Journal of Psychiatry in Medicine*, 1977, *8*(3), 243-255.

Chapter 8

CRISIS INTERVENTION IN COMMUNITY DISASTERS

Theodore Franklin

The emotional effects experienced by disaster victims have been the subject of considerable research and clinical study in recent years. The fact that there are significant emotional impacts associated with disaster sequalae, such as the loss of loved ones and friends, physical injuries, and property loss, has also provided a rich source of morbid fascination for readers, movie-goers, and TV watchers. For example, recent films such as *The Towering Inferno, Earthquake*, and *The Poseiden Adventure*, the television series *Emergency*, and *Paramedic*, and the classic film *San Francisco* depicting an earthquake and its aftermath, continue to attract wide audiences whenever they are shown.

Many if not most people find catastrophes fascinating in that they seek to experience vicariously the anguish of the fictional characters as well as that of real victims described by the news media. Specialists in child development have noted an apparently universal tendency among children at an early age to seek out frightening experiences voluntarily through such things as ghost stories, games which elicit startle responses, and the grisly episodes in classical fairy tales. Developmental psychologists explain that this is a natural and necessary process whereby, early on, we begin to desensitize ourselves to the frightening experiences we inevitably face.

If this desensitizing process is effective, we might expect to find that when one is involved in a disaster, the ability to maintain or regain effective coping behavior often would be evidenced. This is what has been genereally observed by researchers and clinicians working with disaster victims (Quarantelli & Dynes, 1973). This finding runs counter to the popular conception of pervasive gross emotional decompensation as the usual immediate reaction of people who experience a disaster. In other words, the lurid and tragic incidents in which people are trampled to death in attempting to escape a building on fire, as described by Abe (1976), Krim (1976), and Lindemann (1944, 1962), may represent the exception rather than the rule in human responses to major catastrophes.

A question arises as to what does constitute a *crisis* in a disaster in light of the classical conceptualization presented by Caplan (1964). According to Caplan, a crisis involves essentially four aspects: (a) an individual is faced with a unique and stressful event, (b) usual coping strategies are applied in attempting to deal with the event, (c) when these fail other coping strategies are tried, and (d) if none succeed, the individual begins to exhibit a loss of ego integration which may result in long-lasting psychological damage. To what extent this model is applicable to the kinds of emotional problems precipitated by a disaster has not yet been satisfactorily established by research. There is mounting clinical evidence, however, that a disaster may present a different sort of stress from that usually encountered in the personal crisis situation such as that precipitating a suicidal episode (Farberow, 1967).

A disaster is a common stressful event for a large group of individuals. Its impact is communal rather than strictly personal. The people involved in a disaster are responding initially to emergency demands of immediate survival and the saving of lives and property. Much of the behavior occurring during the initial impact and immediately following is more likely to be reflexive in nature, that is, seeking safety, searching for family members and neighbors, digging out demolished structures, and salvaging possessions. At this point in time, the coping measures brought to bear by victims are usually appropriate and effective. It has been found that most victims respond remarkably well, often exhibiting altruistic and heroic actions under disaster-coping pressures (Siporin, 1976).

It is likely, however, that some individuals with marginal personality integration and those who are otherwise under exceptional stress will break down as a consequence of the added impact of a disaster. Long range effects of a disaster on the psychological well-being of survivors have been reported by Titchner and Kapp (1976). However, Murphy (1973) reported that immediately following an earthquake which demolished a psychiatric hospital, some severely disturbed patients regained complete reality contact. They assisted in evacuating other patients, giving directions and assigning tasks. There was what appeared to be "mass shock therapy" for almost all patients, who at least temporarily displayed adaptive behavior.

The prevalence and symptoms of psychic trauma among disaster victims have received considerable attention in the literature. Some authors have theorized or found significant clinical evidence of relatively widespread traumata among survivors (Lifton & Olson, 1976; Rangell, 1976; Wolfenstein, 1957). Immediate or delayed surfacing of psychological problems was seen as a direct effect of the disaster. Other writers have observed that symptoms shown by disaster victims in the immediate postdisaster period were usually normal responses to stress which tended to disappear as time passed and recovery efforts progressed (Taylor, Ross & Quarantelli, 1976). There are also indications that some victims, while apparently not suffering emotional problems directly from the disaster itself, do experience stress related to frustrations and failures in recovery efforts (Hall & Landreth, 1975).

Space does not permit an exhaustive examination of these issues here. Given the many different forms disasters take, the variety of populations at risk, and the wide differences in local response capabilities, the task of developing a single theoretical model or preferred approach for rendering mental health services in disasters appears formidable indeed. At this point a comprehensive service delivery model has not been established. Much more research and clinical knowledge must still be gained. Therefore, the balance of this chapter will focus on the kinds of problems encountered by human services workers in disasters and the ways in which these problems were handled, or might have been better handled.

It might be useful first, however, to offer some background as to who is likely to be responsible for mental health assistance to disaster victims and under what circumstances. Generally, mental health services will be provided under the auspices of local, city, county, and state health departments. Supervisory and treatment personnel will be drawn from community mental health centers, psychiatric hospitals, and local professionals in the community. The bulk of direct service delivery will be carried out by volunteers from the local community who receive training and supervision from professionals in the mental health field. The latter would ordinarily have had prior training and/or experience in disaster work.

The history of formally organized intervention for mental health needs in disasters is relatively brief. Most of the work done by agencies and groups of mental health professionals has occurred within the past decade (Dynes & Quarantelli, 1975). This is not to overlook the invaluable services rendered by various church and interfaith groups, such as the Red Cross, Salvation Army, and other social service agencies. These organizations traditionally have delivered emergency relief services for not only the physical but also the spiritual and psychological needs of disaster victims.

Mental health needs in major disasters were first officially recognized as a significant area of concern in U.S. Public Law 93-288, the 1974 Disaster Relief Act and Amendment. Responsibility for providing training and services was mandated to the National Institute of Mental Health (NIMH) in Sec. 413 of that law, a portion of which reads:

> Crisis counseling assistance and training. The President is authorized (through NIMH) to provide professional counseling services...to victims of major disasters in order to relieve mental health problems caused or aggravated by such disasters... (Public Law 93-288, 1974)

The rationale for the choice of a crisis intervention model in disaster assistance is essentially that when a disaster strikes a crisis is produced. An effective response to that crisis can be based upon experience gained from other applications of crisis intervention. These principles and techniques are aimed at two major goals: (a) to relieve current emotional distress, and (b) to forestall or diminish future emotional difficulties.

The immediate demands of personal survival, rescue of others, and salvage of belongings leave little opportunity for the victim to deal immediately with the emotional impact of the disaster. These affects are typically suppressed or repressed but may be apparent to those trained to observe signs of underlying emotional distress. Experience in working with disaster victims has shown that although most individuals may adequately handle the direct effects of catastrophe, the early provision of crisis services can prevent or lessen the severity of delayed emotional reactions (Jacobsen et al., 1965; McGee, 1973; Morley, 1965). For some individuals with marginal emotional resources, a crisis may aggravate chronic problems or bring about a complete breakdown in coping abilities. Such persons will require intensive and longer term professional intervention to regain their equilibrium.

The nature of the disaster may also play a major role in determining what sort of mental health assistance is needed and possible. Disasters vary in length of warning period, intensity of the catastrophe, duration of impact, number of people involved, extent of property damage, number of casualties, and requirements of the recovery period. Problems encountered as a result of a disaster will also vary according to the type of disaster and size of community involved.

Disasters such as earthquakes, tornadoes, and hurricanes give little or no warning and usually have impacts which are short and sharp. Other disasters such as floods, volcano eruptions, and tidal waves are more likely to give warning and to have impacts of longer duration. If a disaster strikes a large urban community there may be a number of services and trained personnel available for mounting a response. If the disaster strikes a rural area there may be few or no mental health services available (Borgman, 1977).

Historically, phases of disaster have been described in terms of the physical impact of the catastrophe and the responses to it. These divisions are: (a) warning, (b) threat, (c) impact, (d) inventory, (e) rescue, (f) remedy, and (g) recovery (Baker & Chapman, 1962). More recently, Hartsough, Zarle, and Ottinger (1976) have described phases emphasizing the psychological aspects for the victims. These phases are the: (a) heroic, (b) honeymoon, (c) disillusionment, and (d) reconstruction.

The heroic phase occurs at the time of impact and in the period immediately thereafter. Emotions are strong and direct. People find themselves facing and responding to demands for heroic action to save their own and others' lives and property. Altruism is prominent and people expend major energy in helping others to survive and recover. The most important resources during this phase are family groups, neighbors, and emergency relief teams.

The honeymoon phase usually extends from 1 week to 3 to six months after the disaster. For those who have survived, even with the loss of loved ones and possessions, there is a strong sense of having shared with others a dangerous, catastrophic experience and having lived through it. During this period there is often a rush of support from governmental disaster relief agencies and both preexisting and emergent community groups, and promise of much more. The last-mentioned groups develop from the specific needs caused by the disaster and are especially important community resources during this period.

The disillusionment stage usually lasts from about 2 months to 1 or even 2 years. Strong feelings of disappointment, anger, resentment, and bitterness may appear if delay or failures occur and the hopes for and promises of aid are not fulfilled. Outside agencies may withdraw their programs and some of the indigenous community groups may weaken or become nonoperative. Also contributing to this stage may be a gradual loss of feelings of "shared community" as the victims concentrate on rebuilding their own lives and solving their individual problems.

The reconstruction phase, from 6 months to several years after the event, brings with it the realization that the victims will need to solve the problems of rebuilding their own homes, businesses, and lives largely by themselves. They have gradually assumed responsibility for doing so. During this time, new buildings replace those destroyed. There is the development of new programs and plans. These steps serve to reaffirm the victims' belief in their community and in their own capabilities. If this does not occur, the emotional problems which appear may be serious and intense. Community groups with a long-term investment in the community and its people become vital elements in this phase.

In addition to these four phases which may be expected in the course of the disaster and recovery efforts, a number of key concepts have been found to be of major importance in evaluating and providing mental health services (Farberow, 1977).

THE TARGET POPULATION IS PRIMARILY NORMAL

Victims of disasters are generally normal individuals capable of functioning effectively. They have been subjected to severe stress and may be showing signs of emotional strain. This transitory disturbance is to be expected and does not necessarily imply mental illness. People typically do not disintegrate emotionally in response to disaster (Bates et al., 1963; Taylor, Ross, & Quarantelli, 1976). For the most part people perform surprisingly well considering the amount of stress they have to endure. However, frustrations may accumulate, especially as the victims struggle through the subsequent bureaucratic tangle involved in their attempts to secure agency help. Feelings of helplessness and anger may appear. People generally respond to active interest and concern. When workers become individually and personally involved, victims feel an increase in self-esteem. When workers expect healthy responses, pathological responses are less likely to occur.

MENTAL HEALTH LABELS SHOULD BE AVOIDED

Many people are still unable to accept and will even actively refuse help for "emotional problems." The aim of those rendering services should be to provide assistance, compassion, and understanding for problems which are accompanied by emotional strain. It is both inadvisable and inappropriate to use words which imply a need for treatment of mental illness, such as counseling, therapy, psychiatric, neurotic, or psychotic.

HELPING EFFORTS SHOULD BE FLEXIBLE AND INNOVATIVE

Each disaster is unique and requires adaptive responses if help is to be provided most effectively. It is usually necessary to abandon the traditional approaches. More effective help can be made available with outreach procedures involving case findings in the community and at disaster relief centers (Heffron, 1977).

PROGRAMS MUST RELY ON COMMUNITY RESOURCES

For the local citizens, the sense of participation and influence in decision making in recovery is extremely useful. Selection of human services workers, both professional and nonprofessional, from the community in which the disaster occurred has an additional advantage for the workers themselves. When victims of a disaster are able to be active and to participate fully in reconstructive activities, recovery is much quicker and the long-term effects less serious. For detailed information on the selection and training of volunteer disaster workers, the reader is referred to the NIMH Training Manual for Human Services Workers in Major Disasters (Farberow, 1978). The research team responsible for the development of this manual participated in the mental health response to the Teton Dam disaster which occurred in Idaho Falls, June 5, 1976. It is chiefly from these experiences that the following examples of disaster crisis intervention are drawn.

The most commonly found thoughts, feelings, and behaviors of disaster victims are: (a) concern for basic survival, (b) grief over the loss of loved ones or loss of prized possessions, (c) separation anxiety, often expressed as fear for safety of significant others, (d) regressive behavior, e.g., reappearance of thumbsucking and fear of darkness among children, (e) relocation and isolation anxieties, (f) need to express feelings about experiences during the disaster, (g) need to feel one is a part of the community and its rehabilitation efforts, and (h) altruism and desire to help others.

It has also been found that there are special groups among disaster victims who represent more than average vulnerability in the disaster as well as its after-effects. For example, the very young and the elderly have been found to present serious physical and emotional disablements following a disaster (Newman, 1976; Poulschok & Cohen, 1975). Some ethnic and subcultural groups may suffer excessively or needlessly because of communication limitations or a disinclination to avail themselves of community rehabilitation assistance

(Gomez, 1976). For further information on the identification and provision of services for special risk groups among disaster victims, the reader is again referred to the NIMH Training Manual (Farberow, 1978).

Among the types of disaster-related emotional problems most frequently encountered are: (a) depression, (b) grief, (c) anger, (d) guilt, (e) apathy, (f) fears, (g) the burn-out syndrome, (h) bizarre behavior, and (i) suicide. Following are examples of cases involving these reactions.

DEPRESSION

A field worker finds a middle-aged man pacing up and down in front of his flood-ravaged home. Some of the water-soaked furniture has been dragged into the yard to dry out. The man has apparently abandoned further attempts to salvage his furnishings and is now pacing about aimlessly in what remains of his front yard. This illustration of depression differs from the popular conception of a depressed person who exhibits severe apathy, withdrawal, and disinterest in what is going on around him. In this example, the depression is masked by or expressed in agitated activity which is nonproductive. Unless the depression in this phase is recognized and dealt with, it may progress to more serious mental and physical symptoms.

Assistance for the person in this instance might take the form of verbal reassurance and acknowledgement of the emotional distress experienced by the victim. Attempts might be made to offer help in salvaging belongings, by providing a respite with hot coffee or tea, or simply conversing with the individual about the disaster and its direct effects on his life.

GRIEF

A man appears in a one-stop disaster relief center in a small western city severely damaged by an earthquake. The man asks for help in acquiring a set of mechanic's tools which he needs for his work. His set was lost along with all the rest of his belongings in the earthquake and susequent fire. While giving the required information to the disaster relief worker, the man mentions that his son was killed in the earthquake.

The man appears to be in complete control of his emotions and seems to be going about the business of reestablishing his life in a well-organized but perhaps too expeditious manner. Such behavior would ordinarily be considered healthy following a suitable period of mourning. In this instance there had been no apparent mourning. The father was busying himself with constructive tasks to screen the emotional pain and to avoid dealing directly with the loss of his son. It might be expected that at some point in the near future the father would become overwhelmed by the emotions he had been trying to suppress.

Attempting to intervene with unsolicited mental health service in such an instance presents complex problems for the worker. A cautious, sensitive, and innovative approach would seem indicated. Perhaps a brief, gentle comment about the loss is as much as would be immediately appropriate. Efforts might be directed to establishing a helping relationship with the bereaved father and awaiting another opportunity to deal more directly with the loss. Effective assistance might take the form of dealing with insurance matters, making arrangements for the burial, and notifying relatives of the tragedy and funeral details, thus alerting them to the father's need for emotional support. This situation is a good example of the way the traditional role of the mental health worker may require expansion and redirection in rendering assistance.

ANGER

A rural valley with many small farms was devastated when a newly finished dam gave way and flooded the area below it. Some citizens who had suffered losses in the flood were observed throwing rocks at trucks belonging to the construction company which had worked on the dam. Anger was also expressed by local relief workers whose efforts were hampered by bureaucratic red tape. Victims exhibited anger toward relief workers both for interfering with their lives and also for not doing enough to help them.

Anger is a natural and often expected reaction to adversity. The degree of anger felt and ways in which it is expressed are related to both internal and external factors. In this case anger was expressed toward those whom the victims held responsible for the dam's failure. Anger was also no doubt derived from feelings of personal helplessness to prevent or repair the damages of the disaster.

Nonprofessionals frequently find it particularly difficult to deal with anger in a therapeutic manner. The trained worker is aware of the value of permitting or encouraging some initial ventilation rather than immediately attempting to placate or divert the anger. It is difficult for the inexperienced worker to deal with his/her own anxiety when exposed to angry outbursts and the perhaps righteous wrath of the disaster victim.

GUILT

A woman whose home miraculously escaped flood damage appears at the local health center with various physical symptoms including stomach cramps, loss of appetite, and severe headaches. Medical examination fails to find a physical basis for the complaints and the woman is referred to a mental health worker. During consultation with a psychologist it is learned that the home of a close friend and neighbor was completely destroyed by the flood. The worker helps the woman to accept the unpredictable nature of the disaster which ruins one person's home and spares that of a near neighbor. Her feelings of guilt and their accompanying physical symptoms are lessened and she is able to extend a welcomed assistance to her neighbor in coping with her loss.

Guilt is a frequent occurrence among survivors of a disaster. We all experience to some degree the uneasiness which accompanies sudden good fortune while others close to us suffer tragic loss. Our own sense of self worth is called into question. In these instances the worker's intervention is primarily that of providing the victim an opportunity to confront directly these natural human reactions.

APATHY

An elderly man owned and operated a small private fishing lake and boat rental concession at his homesite. A flood destroyed his boats and equipment and completely filled the lake with mud. The old man, who lived alone, is discovered by neighbors several weeks later. He has taken to his bed, neglecting to eat or care for himself. At the time he is found, his weight and physical condition have deteriorated to the point where he is barely alive. At first he refused any assistance. However, those who found him persist and eventually remove him to a hospital. Although he initially recovers from the debilitation, he dies shortly after being placed in a residence for the elderly.

In disasters, apathy is frequently found among the elderly who suffer significant losses of possessions, homes, friends, and neighbors. There are feelings, often realistic, that they will not again be able to recover or replace these losses. There is limited capacity for readjustment to new and strange surroundings. Intervention in such cases should begin as soon as possible and emphasize concrete forms of assistance. Relatives and friends should be located and alerted if possible. If relocation is necessary it should be as near as possible to a place which is familiar to the older disaster victim. If possible, picture albums and other momentos should be located and sent along.

FEARS

An otherwise normal 6-year-old girl who has experienced a severe earthquake becomes terrified and cries when a heavy truck passes by the house causing it to shake. A 4-year-old boy, who was suddenly evacuated just before a flood destroyed his home, develops the habit of sleeping with all his clothes on and with his remaining belongings packed in a suitcase at the foot of his bed. A 7-year-old boy, who survived a flood caused by a torrential rain, is found crying and crouched under a stairwell when a light rain starts to fall.

These persisting fears are sometimes found among young children and occasionally adolescents and adults following a disaster. They are technically referred to as traumatic neuroses. With most otherwise healthy persons such fears tend to subside as time passes. If they continue for weeks or months after the disaster it is apparent that the intervention of professional mental health specialists is required. Much can be done, however, in the immediate postdisaster period to relieve these symptoms and to prevent their continued self-reinforcement.

Talking with the child in a gentle, reassuring manner is helpful. Permitting or encouraging the child to talk about what is frightening and to verbally relive the experience is also extremely valuable. Creative games in which the disaster is relived help the child to develop a feeling of mastery over the event. Adolescents and adults who display recurrent fear symptoms should be permitted to relive the experience verbally, to become actively involved in recovery efforts, and to learn more about the causes and means of possible protection from future disasters. These steps have been found to be particularly valuable in fostering a sense of personal control in essentially uncontrollable events.

THE BURN-OUT SYNDROME

Two police officers are on duty at a checkpoint for autos entering the disaster area. It is their job to permit only those to enter who have homes or business in the area, and those involved in relief activities. There is a constant stream of vehicles lined up in both directions. The officers must take the time to inspect identification and passes, answer questions about disaster recovery activities, reassure anxious homeowners, and placate angry residents frustrated at the delay in reaching their homes. These officers have had 12 to 15-hour duty days in the week immediately following the disaster. Their faces show fatigue; their efficiency is at a low ebb. One officer describes his concern about his family to a relief worker. Another officer is anxious about all the work that needs to be done at his house.

These men exhibit excessive fatigue, irritability, anxiety, impatience; all symptoms of the "burn-out syndrome." Front-line workers typically overextend themselves during and following disasters. This most often occurs when there are few or no replacements. Sometimes, however, even when replacements are available, conscientious workers refuse relief and push themselves beyond effective limits. Such action might seem altruistic and commendable. In reality, the tired and inefficient relief worker can become more of a liability than an asset in rescue and recovery operations. These workers are frequently called upon to make critical and sometimes life-saving decisions. The worker experiencing burn-out may wind up doing more harm than good. Additionally, the worker may fail to recognize these signs in himself or herself although they may be obvious to others. It is primarily the responsibility of those supervising the front-line relief workers to ensure that those experiencing burn-out are relieved from their duties if at all possible.

BIZARRE BEHAVIOR

A man whose entire herd of cattle was lost in a flood is apprehended shooting his neighbor's surviving cattle. The man can offer no rational explanation for his behavior.

Sometimes the effects of a disaster prove to be an overwhelming experience for the victim. The excessive stress causes a breakdown of usually effective coping behavior. The individual exhibits irrational or bizarre behavior. Contrary to popular conception, this is an unusual occurrence during disasters. Individuals who suffer emotional breakdowns are generally those who have a history of prior emotional disturbance. It is valuable for local mental health workers to be aware of those who are at special risk during an emergency situation. Immediate admittance to a hospital or attention from a professional mental health specialist is indicated for those who display aberrant or potentially dangerous behavior.

SUICIDE

A woman who lives alone is found dead of a self-inflicted gunshot wound following a flood which devastated her community.

Similarly to psychotic episodes, suicide is not a common occurrence among disaster victims. Again, one of the advantages of recruiting local personnel for disaster services is that it increases the likelihood that persons at high risk in the community will be already known to the workers. Immediate and precautionary interventions might thus be made with the possibility of forestalling tragic incidents.

The above examples are typical of many of the mental health problems found in disasters. These anecdotal descriptions, however, do not deal specifically with the question of frequency of occurrences. Experience gained in dealing with disaster victims does suggest that an outreach approach offers greater scope and effectiveness than does the traditional treatment model. As indicated earlier in this chapter, the field of disaster intervention is still new, with most of the formal research and clinical work conducted during the past decade.

INFORMATION SOURCES ON DISASTER EFFECTS

Among those who have contributed greatly to our current understanding of mental health problems encountered in disasters is Howard. J. Parad who worked with one of the early founders of crisis theory, Gerald Caplan. Recently Parad coedited a book which compiled most of the information currently available on the mental health aspects of disasters (Parad, Resnik, & Parad, 1976).

The best known source of information about disasters is the Disaster Research Center at Ohio State University, directed by E. L. Quarantelli. Most important has been the establishment of a section in the National Institute of Mental Health, the Disaster Assistance and Emergency Mental Health Section, whose first director was Calvin J. Fredrick and is now headed by Mary Lystad. The section serves to coordinate professional mental health interest and research activities in the area, to stimulate training of professional, paraprofessional, and volunteer personnel, and to facilitate the establishment and funding of disaster mental health services.

In summary, the provision of disaster mental health services is a relatively recent occurrence. There has been to date an emphasis on sociological, demographic, and statistical quantification of disasters. Clinical identification of and intervention with disaster-related emotional problems are reported less often in the literature (Frederick, 1977). This does not suggest a lack of interest in this area by clinical-research and treatment personnel. These activities must typically await the actual occurrence of a disaster and active involvement by professional mental health specialists. Predisaster training and consultation by those with experience in the field have been relatively limited and represent an area in which much more needs to be done.

It is important for professionals and nonprofessionals alike to be aware of the details of Public Law 93-288. It is also important to become acquainted with funding procedures in the event of an emergency (NIMH, Disaster Assistance and Emergency Mental Health, 1976). The timely award of funds can spell the difference between mental health services which are adequate, limited, or altogether absent.

REFERENCES

Abe, K. The behavior of survivors and victims in a Japanese nightclub fire. *Mass Emergencies*, 1976, *1*, 119-124.

Baker, G., & Chapman, D. *Man and society in disaster*. N.Y.: Basic Books, Inc., 1962.

Bates F., et al. *The social and psychological consequences of a natural disaster: A longitudinal study of Hurricane Audrey*. Washington, D.C.: National Academy of Sciences-National Research Council, 1963.

Borgman, R. Crisis intervention in rural community disasters. *Social Casework*, 1977, *58*, 562-567.

Dynes, R., & Quarantelli, E. The delivery of mental health services in the Xenia Tornado. Final Report from the Disaster Research Center, Ohio State University, to the Ohio Department of Mental Health and Retardation, June 30, 1975.

Caplan, G. *Principles of preventive psychiatry*. N.Y.: Basic Books, 1964.

Farberow, N. Crisis, disaster and suicide: Theory and therapy. In E. Shneidman (Ed.), *Essays in self-destruction*. N.Y.: Science House, 1967.

Farberow, N. Mental health response in major disasters. *The Psychotherapy Bulletin*, 1977, *109*, 10-19.

Farberow, N. (Ed.) *Training manual for human service workers in major disasters*. DHEW Publication No. (ADM) 77-538, Washington, D.C.: Superintendent of Documents, U.S. Government Printing Office, Stock No. 017-024-0685., 1978.

Frederick, C. Current thinking about crisis or psychological intervention in U.S. disasters. *Mass Emergencies*, 1977, *2*, 43-50.

Gomez, A. Some considerations in structuring human services for the Spanish-speaking population of the United States. *International Journal of Mental Health*, 1976, *5*, 60-68.

Hall, P., & Landreth, P. Assessing some long-term consequences of a natural disaster. *Mass Emergencies*, 1975, *1*, 55-62.

Hartsough, D., Zarle, T., & Ottinger, D. Rapid response to disaster: The Monticello Tornado. In H. Parad, H. Resnik, & L. Parad (Eds.), *Emergency and disaster management: A mental health sourcebook*. Bowie, Maryland: The Charles Press, 1976.

Heffron, E. Project Outreach: Crisis intervention following natural disaster. *Journal of Community Psychology*, 1977, *5*, 103-111.

Jacobsen, G., et al. The scope and practice of an early-access brief treatment psychiatric center. *American Journal of Psychiatry*, 1965, *121*, 1176-1182.

Krim, A. Urban disaster: Victims of fire. In H. Parad, H. Resnik, & L. Parad (Eds.), *Emergency and disaster management: A mental health sourcebook*. Bowie, Maryland: The Charles Press, 1976.

Lifton, R., & Olson, E. The human meaning of total disaster: The Buffalo Creek experience. *Psychiatry*, 1976, *39*, 1-18.

Lindemann, E. Symptomatology and management of acute grief. *American Journal of Psychiatry*, 1944, *101*, 141-148.

Lindemann, E. Preventive intervention in situational crises. *Clinical Psychology*, 1962, *4*, 69-88.

McGee, R. The role of crisis intervention services in disaster recovery. Center for Crisis Intervention Research, Gainesville, Florida, University of Florida, 1973.

Morley, W. Treatment of the patient in crisis. *Western Medicine*, 1965, *3*, 77.

Murphy, L. San Fernando Valley, California Earthquake of February 9, 1971. Washington, D.C.: U.S. Department of Commerce, 1973.

Newman, J. Children of disaster: Clinical observations at Buffalo Creek. *American Journal of Psychiatry*, 1976, *133*, 306-312.

Parad, H., Resnik, H., & Parad, L. (Eds.), *Emergency and disaster management: A mental health source book*. Bowie, Maryland: The Charles Press, 1976.

Poulschok, S., & Cohen, E. The elderly in the aftermath of a disaster. *Gerontologist*, 1975, *15*, 357 - 361.

Quarantelli, E., & Dynes. R. Images of disaster behavior: Myths and consequences. Columbus, Ohio: Disaster Research Center, Ohio State University, 1973.

Rangell, L. Discussion of the Buffalo Creek Disaster: The course of psychic trauma. *American Journal of Psychiatry*, 1976, *133*, 313-316.

Siporin, M. Altriuism, disaster, and crisis intervention. In H. Parad, H. Resnik, & L. Parad (Eds.), *Emergency and disaster management: A mental health sourcebook*. Bowie, Maryland: The Charles Press, 1976.

Taylor, V., Ross, G., & Quarantelli, E. Delivery of mental health services in disaster: The Xenia Tornado and some implications. *Monograph* #11, Columbus, Ohio: The Ohio State University, 1976.

Titchner, J., & Kapp, F. Family and character change at Buffalo Creek. *American Journal of Psychiatry*, 1976, *133*, 295-299.

Wolfenstein, M. *Disaster: A psychological essay.* Glencoe, Illinois: The Falcon's Wing Press and Free Press, 1957.

Chapter 9

TREATMENT FOR
RAPE-RELATED PROBLEMS:
Crisis Intervention Is Not Enough

Dean G. Kilpatrick
Lois J. Veronen

Within the past few years, increased attention has been focused upon sexual assault. There has been a dramatic increase in the number of reported rapes; according to data from the FBI Uniform Crime Reports, the number of rapes increased from 37,900 in 1970 to 63,020 in 1977, an increase of 166%.

Laws have been changed. New statutes define rape as a type of assault rather than a crime of passion. Punishment for the crime is frequently based on the degree of force or threat of force used. Now, a victim's sexual history wih men other than the defendant is not admissible as evidence.

Medical services have been expanded. In most hospital emergency rooms, a rape victim can obtain an evidence-gathering exam and receive treatment for protection against venereal disease and pregnancy.

In addition, a victim's psychological trauma is recognized. Rape crisis centers, hospital social services, and mental health centers are seeking information and training in order to provide counseling and treatment for the victim and her family. Unfortunately, as we have concluded elsewhere (Kilpatrick, Resick, & Veronen, 1981; Kilpatrick, Veronen, & Resick, 1979a, 1979b), there is relatively little information available from methodologically sound research regarding the effects of rape or treatment of rape-related problems.

Although much of the methodologically sound research is in progress, we do have considerable information based on relatively unsystematic research (e.g., Burgess & Holmstrom, 1974a). This research describes rape as a crisis and also describes crisis counseling with rape victims. Burgess and Holmstrom's work has been most influential, and their crisis theory conceptualization of rape and its effects has had a major impact upon the treatment of rape victims.

During the past 9 years, we have worked with rape victims as members of People Against Rape, a Charleston, South Carolina rape crisis center. For the past 6 years, we have conducted research on rape effects and the efficacy of treatment procedures for rape-related problems via the Sexual Assault Research Project, funded by the National Center for the Prevention and Control of Rape.* Clinical and research experience has led us to conclude that crisis theory and crisis intervention have major weaknesses. We have developed a social learning model which explains the effects of a rape experience and have developed behavioral treatment procedures for rape-related problems. We contend that these social learning conceptualizations and behavioral treatment procedures have several advantages over crisis conceptualizations and interventions. While undoubtedly useful, crisis intervention is not enough.

In the remainder of this chapter, we will first present a brief overview and critique of crisis theory. Next, we will describe the victim's perception of a sexual assault experience and how this experience has been conceptualized using crisis theory. An alternative social learning conceptualization of a rape experience also will be presented. The final portion of the chapter will deal with crisis intervention and behavioral approaches for treatment of rape-related problems.

---

*The Sexual Assault Research Project at the Medical University of South Carolina, for which the authors are co-principal investigators, is supported by National Center for the Prevention and Control of Rape Grant No. R01 MH29602, which began in April, 1977 and continues through June, 1983. Data reported in this chapter were collected for that project.

CRISIS THEORY AND INTERVENTION

An Overview

Modern crisis theory is based on the work of several authors (Butcher & Maudal, 1976; Caplan, 1961, 1964; Schulberg & Sheldon, 1968; Taplin, 1971). Korchin (1976) states that crisis theory is more. of a general orientation than a well-developed theory. Butcher and Maudal (1976) provide an excellent summary of the general assumptions of crisis theory. The first assumption is that crisis is a state characterized by high levels of subjective discomfort or distress and the inability to effectively modify the source of stress which produced the crisis. A second assumption is that crisis reactions can be produced by a variety of stressful life situations. A third assumption is that those situations which are cognitively appraised as dangerous or harmful will be more likely to provoke a crisis response. The individual's appraisal of his or her capacity to cope with the situations is also important (i.e., those who think they can cope with a given situation are less likely to have a crisis reaction than those who doubt their ability to cope). A fourth assumption is that some events, such as the death of a spouse, natural disasters, and serious illness, have a high probability of producing crisis in most people. In fact, the existence of an easily discernible stressful life event in the life of a distressed individual is *the* key factor in differentiating crisis reactions from other, more psychopathological responses. A fifth assumption is that crisis reactions are presumptively time-limited. The crisis is resolved, either adaptively or maladaptively, within a fairly limited period of time, usually 6 to 8 weeks (Bloom, 1963). Implicit is an overriding assumption that crisis theory approaches are most appropriately used with relatively normal individuals responding to environmental stress with which they are temporarily unable to cope rather than with chronically maladjusted individuals with significant psychopathology.

With respect to crisis intervention, it has been observed that "crisis intervention techniques are loosely organized and cover a wide range of procedures" (Auerbach & Kilmann, 1977, p. 1190). Auerbach and Kilmann summarize the general factors in crisis intervention approaches as: (a) focusing upon resolution of immediate problems instead of restructuring basic personality, (b) consisting of a minimal number of brief contacts, and (c) containing a high level of therapist activity which marshals human and agency resources facilitating client readjustment. Other important features of crisis intervention approaches include: (a) an emphasis on helping the person in crisis identify coping strategies and engage in problem-solving behavior, and (b) an attempt to avoid fostering dependency on the therapist. Given these rather general principles, it is predictable that there is considerable variation among the actual procedures labeled as crisis intervention.

Crisis Theory: A Brief Critique

Auerbach and Kilmann's (1977) review of the literature indicates that crisis theory and intervention programs based on the theory are enormously popular. Therefore, it is important to examine the theory's strengths and weaknesses.

A major strength is that crisis approaches avoid the limitations of psychoanalytic trait theories. Trait theories are based on an assumption that enduring characteristics or behavior patterns are formed early in childhood and persist throughout life. If an individual is experiencing distress, the assumption would be generally made that distress is an outward manifestation of inner conflict resulting from the interplay of enduring psychological drives and traits. Treatment efforts would focus primarily on uncovering these long-standing conflicts. Some psychoanalytic theorists (e.g., Deutsch, 1944; Factor, 1954) have suggested that certain women have an unconscious desire to be raped and actually provoke their attacks! Clearly, trait approaches are not particularly well-suited conceptually to deal with the impact of a sudden traumatic event and its effect upon a "normal," nonpsychopathological person. Therefore, crisis intervention, with its assumption of the relative normality of its clients and its primary focus on present problems rather than psychosexual development, is a considerable improvement over traditional psychoanalytic trait approaches. Furthermore, there have been no known instances in which crisis intervention theorists have accused victims of provoking their attack.

A second strength of crisis intervention is that it is relatively simple to teach and learn, at least in comparison with long- or short-term psychotherapy. Auerbach and Kilmann's (1977) review provides numerous examples of how the technique has been used by professionals and paraprofessionals with a variety of client groups. Assuming that it is effective, the fact that crisis intervention can be conducted by paraprofessionals and that it is time-limited would make it an extremely cost effective treatment approach.

In addition to its considerable strengths, crisis theory has major conceptual and empirical weaknesses. Elsewhere (Kilpatrick, Veronen, & Resick, 1982) we have observed that crisis theory is circular in the definitions of its major terms and imprecise in its predictions. A "crisis state" is inferred from the observation of distressed behavior. The existence of the "crisis state" is *a priori* evidence that "coping skills" have been unsuccessful in dealing with a stressful life event. When the distressed or disrupted behavior diminishes, we infer that the "crisis state" has been resolved, that equilibrium has been reestablished, and that "coping skills" are now operative. The only aspect of the crisis theory model which is readily observable and not a hypothetical construct is the client's overt behavior and/or subjective report of his or her psychological state. Other components in the theory, such as crisis state, coping skills, and crisis resolution, are hypothetical constructs which are inferred on the basis of changes in the client's behavior. Thus, the circularity of crisis theory and lack of empirical definition of important components represents a weakness. It is reasonable to ask the question: Why not focus directly and entirely on the behavior(s) *per se* rather than invoking such a vague concept as a crisis state?

A third major weakness of crisis theory is that there is little empirical support for one major aspect of the theory, the notion that distress diminishes significantly within 6 to 8 weeks after the onset of the crisis. Although this issue has received scant research attention, a recent study (Lewis, Gottesman, & Gutstein, 1979) assessed anxiety, depression, self-esteem, and locus of control in two groups of patients. A crisis group was to undergo exploratory surgery to determine if they had cancer. A noncrisis group was to undergo minor surgery. Crisis and noncrisis groups were tested immediately before and at 2, 5, and 8 weeks after the surgery. The crisis group experienced more distress than the noncrisis group, but, contrary to prediction, the crisis group's anxiety and depression *increased* over the 8-week postsurgery period. Similarly, data from our Sexual Assault Research Project (e.g., Kilpatrick et al., 1981; Kilpatrick et al., 1979a, 1979b;

Veronen & Kilpatrick, in press) indicate that rape victims' distress diminishes somewhat at 3 months postrape but remains significantly elevated at 1 year postrape.

A fourth major weakness of crisis intervention is that its efficacy as a treatment procedure has not been extensively evaluated. Auerbach and Kilmann's (1978) review concluded that few studies attempted any sort of evaluation of crisis intervention's efficacy and even fewer were methodologically adequate. In fact, the absence of any outcome research on crisis intervention's effects with rape victims was specifically noted.

RAPE AND SEXUAL ASSAULT

Definition

There are a variety of perspectives from which sexual assault or rape can be viewed. Some individuals make a distinction between rape and sexual assault, defining sexual assault as forced or coerced sexual activity which does not involve intercourse. We use the terms interchangeably. Legal definitions of rape have changed substantially and vary considerably from state to state. There are considerable differences among cultures and societies, both in how rape is defined and in how frequently it occurs. Feminist definitions of rape have focused upon rape as a political act. Brownmiller (1975) in particular states that rape is an act of power and that fear of rape is a vehicle through which men control women in the battle of the sexes. Several research studies are in progress or have been completed which are attempting to determine under what circumstances a situation is labeled as rape (e.g., Goodchilds, Note 1; Koss, Note 2; Selby, Note 3).

In spite of the complexities in defining rape, definitional issues can be simplified. Since we are interested in providing services to victims, the victim's perspective on her assault is more important than what the law says about whether a rape "legally" occurred. Her experiences and perceptions of the rape itself are the most important determinants of her psychological response to the rape.

We define rape as any nonconsentual sexual activity which is obtained through coercion, force, or threat of force (Veronen & Kilpatrick, 1983). If a woman considers herself to have been forced to have nonconsentual sexual activity, we consider her to be a victim.

The Victim's Perspective

From the victim's perspective, rape is a terrifying, potentially life-threatening event. We asked victims to identify symptoms they experienced during the rape itself (Veronen, Kilpatrick, & Resick, 1979), and the results of these ratings suggest that victims experience symptoms of profound anxiety during the rape. Victims reported feeling worried (96%), scared (96%), terrified (92%), confused (92%), and experienced such physiological symptoms as shaking or trembling (96%), racing heart (84%), pain (72%), rapid breathing (64%), tight muscles (68%), and numbness (60%). Victims also reported feeling anger (80%), shame-humiliation (72%), and helplessness (88%). Most victims stated they were afraid of being killed (Veronen & Kilpatrick, 1983). There is considerable agreement that terror, fear of being hurt or even killed, loss of control, and sense of personal violation are the most salient aspects of the rape situation for the victim (Bard & Sangrey, 1979; Burgess & Holmstrom, 1974b; Kilpatrick et al., 1982; Veronen & Kilpatrick, in press).

Termination of the rape does not eliminate stress for the victim. Victims confront a variety of difficult decisions, two of which are whether to report the assault and whom to tell about their experience. A decision to report the assault to law enforcement authorities sets into motion a chain of events which requires the victim to interact with various agents of the health care delivery and criminal justice systems. If she decides to tell family members and/or friends about her attack, she faces potential censure resulting from generally negative attitudes about rape victims held by the general population (Burt, Note 4). Moreover, rape is a real threat to the self-esteem of the victim since she has grown up believing that nice women don't get raped and that women who are raped must be "asking for it" in some way (Veronen & Kilpatrick, Note 5). When a woman becomes a victim, there is a strong tendency for her to blame herself for the assault and to suffer reductions in self-esteem.

Crisis Theory Conceptualizations

It is not surprising that crisis theory has been used to explain the victim's reactions to rape. Burgess and Holmstrom (1974a) titled their influential book *Rape: Victims of Crisis*, and they state that rape produces a disruption in the victim's "physical, emotional, social and sexual equilibrium" (p. 109) and, therefore, represents a crisis. Bard and Sangrey (1979), who have conducted research with victims of several types of crimes, suggest that personal crime in general and rape in particular are extremely stressful. Bard and Sangrey note that criminals usually strike without warning, which precludes any preparation by victims and reduces the probability that they can cope with overwhelming stress resulting from an unexpected, dangerous assault.

Burgess and Holmstrom (1974b) state that victims experience a variety of symptoms in response to the stress of a rape experience and have labeled these symptoms the rape trauma syndrome. As they describe it, the rape trauma syndrome has two states: (a) an immediate or acute phase, and (b) a long-term reorganization phase. In the acute phase, victims are described as experiencing considerable disorganization of behavior and disruption in life style. Physical reactions, emotional reactions, and disturbed thoughts which are said to occur during this phase could readily be viewed as comprising a crisis state. Burgess and Holmstrom (1974a) are rather vague about the duration of this acute phase, stating only that it "may last a few days to a few weeks" (p. 41).

In their description of the long-term reorganization phase, Burgess and Holmstrom (1974b) stress the fact that rape forces the victim to cope with a variety of things in the long as well as the short term. Among the long-term changes noted were changes in life style, increases in frequency of disturbing dreams and nightmares, and development of rape-related phobias. The length of this phase is not precisely defined although a recent book on long-term "recovery" from rape by Burgess and Holmstrom (1979) suggests that it may take years for "recovery" to occur and that some victims may never achieve their pre-rape level of functioning.

Bard and Sangrey (1979) state that crime victims go through three stages in the resolution of their crime-induced crisis reactions:

(a) an impact state, (b) a recoil stage, and (c) a reorganization phase. The impact stage is similar to Burgess and Holmstrom's (1974b) acute phase.

During the recoil phase, victims are described as experiencing a variety of strong emotions and, at different times, attempting to deal with the feelings by denying them. Bard and Sangrey (1979) contend that some amount of denial is necessary if the crime victim is to adjust to the enormity of what has happened. A great deal of emotional lability can also be expected, with victims feeling one day that they are on top of things and feeling the next that they can't cope at all.

Bard and Sangrey (1979) see the reorganization phase as the period when the victim assimilates the victimization experience, experiences less intense emotions about it, puts the victimization in proper perspective, and goes on with his or her life. Like Burgess and Holmstrom, Bard and Sangrey do not give precise information about the length of each phase or about how to determine which phase an individual is in at any given time.

Sutherland and Scherl (1970) stated that response to rape probably consists of three phases: (a) acute reaction, (b) outward adjustment with denial, and (c) integration and resolution. These three phases are described essentially the same as those of Bard and Sangrey (1979).

It should also be noted that these crisis theory conceptualizations of rape effects are speculative rather than based on empirical research. Burgess and Holmstrom's (1974a, 1974b) work was based on interviews done with rape victims, but, as has been discussed elsewhere (Resick, Kilpatrick, & Veronen, Note 6), their research is replete with serious methodological problems. Bard and Sangrey (1979) admit that their work is not based on research but rather on informal contact with crime victims. Sutherland and Scherl's (1970) observations were based on interviews with 13 victims. Thus, these crisis theorists have provided rich anecdotal data about the effects of rape but their work is not as strong as it might be methodologically.

There are problems with the notion of phases or stages of response to rape. If a phase is to be useful, its characteristics should be defined precisely. The criteria for classification should also be defined empirically. If we know a victim's symptoms or behavior patterns at a given point in time, then we should be able to classify her into the appropriate phase or stage. Additionally, knowing what stage or phase she is in should provide us with some useful information about appropriate treatment or prognosis. Unless the behaviors, symptoms, treatment procedures, and/or prognoses of victims differ for each phase or stage, it is reasonable to question the value of having stages.

Social Learning Theory Conceptualizations

Given the victim's feelings of terror, extreme anxiety, and helplessness during the rape, several aspects of social learning theory can be used to predict development of rape-related problems. Elsewhere (e.g., Kilpatrick, Veronen, & Resick, 1977; Kilpatrick et al., 1979a, 1979b; Kilpatrick et al., 1982; Veronen & Kilpatrick, 1980), we have presented our social learning theory of how rape-related problems develop, and below we summarize the highlights of this theory.

Rape can be viewed as a classical conditioning situation in which the threat of being killed or physically harmed, pain, and lack of control are unconditioned stimuli which produce unconditioned responses of anxiety. Through the process of classical conditioning, any stimuli present during the attack become conditioned stimuli which are capable of evoking conditioned responses of fear and anxiety. Thus, events present at the time of the rape acquire the capacity to evoke fear and anxiety. Moreover, persons, situations, or events similar to these conditioned stimuli can also evoke anxiety because of stimulus generalization. Thus, the victim fears not only the rapist (a quite reasonable fear!) but may also fear men who have characteristics similar to the rapist. Similarly, since sexual activity is involved in rape, it is reasonable to expect cues for sexual behavior to evoke anxiety in victims.

Several predictions follow from the theory (Kilpatrick et al., 1979b). First, victims should be more fearful and anxious than nonvictims. Second, analysis of situations feared by victims should reveal the presence of rape-related conditioned stimuli. Finally, because there is a tendency to make avoidance responses when a rape-related conditioned stimulus is encountered, fear and anxiety should be relatively long-term problems for victims.

Victims might be expected to become depressed as well. Seligman's (1975) learned helplessness model states that depression is likely to develop when individuals are placed in aversive situations where their behavior has no effect on outcomes. The feelings of helplessness and loss of control reported by rape victims suggest that rape may produce depression through learned helplessness. Rape-induced avoidance behavior and an overall reduction in the rate of behavior appears to occur among rape victims. Lewinsohn (1974) believes that depression occurs because of a lowered rate of response-contingent positive reinforcement, and lowering the rate of behavior reduces opportunities for positive reinforcement. Therefore, rape might produce depression through this mechanism. Finally, cognitive theories of depression (Beck, 1976) place great emphasis upon the role of negative self-evaluation. Victims are not immune to rape myths which permeate our society and may often feel that they have either done something to bring on their attack or are being punished for their past behavior. Additionally, victims often feel worthless and ashamed. Thus, victims may develop depression because of faulty cognitions and/or negative self-statements.

In summary, our social learning model predicts that fear, anxiety, depression, and sexual dysfunction should be major problems for rape victims. What empirical support exists for the theory?

In our Sexual Assault Research Project, we are evaluating the effects of rape longitudinally by assessing recent rape victims and a comparison group of nonvictims at several postrape intervals. Our research is focused primarily on fear and anxiety, but the assessment battery measures a broad range of mood states, symptoms, and behaviors. In summary, these have been our major findings. Victims report experiencing considerable anxiety, fear, and helplessness during the rape itself (Veronen et al., 1979). At 6-21 days and 1 month postrape, victims experience generalized distress and disruption of behavior (Kilpatrick et al., 1979a). Victims were significantly more disturbed on 25 of 28 assessment measures. However by 3 months postrape, generalized distress has diminished such that victims and nonvictims differ primarily on measures of fear and anxiety. The 6 month postrape assessment yielded similar findings, as did the 1 year postrape assessment (Kilpatrick et al., 1981). These findings suggest that there is some improvement by 3 months post-rape but that fear and anxiety remain rather high for at least a year after the assault. Examination of items and situations rated as disturbing by victims but not by nonvictims revealed that such fears were rape-related in that they were rape cues, rape-precipitated concerns, and/or cues signaling vulnerability to subsequent attack (Kilpatrick et al., 1979b). Not all women are functioning poorly a year afer their assault, however. We found that approximately 20% of the victims in our study were relatively symptom free at the 1 year assessment (Veronen & Kilpatrick, in press).

Other researchers are investigating the incidence of depression among rape victims (Calhoun, Atkeson, & Resick, Note 7; Frank, Turner, & Duffy, 1979). Preliminary data from these investigators suggest that there is an increased incidence of depression among victims. Similarly, one recent study (Feldman-Summers, Gordon, & Meagher, 1979) found that rape decreased victims' rated satisfaction with a variety of sexual behaviors. In a current study specifically investigating sexual dysfunction among victims and the efficacy of treatment procedures for such problems, Becker (Note 8) is finding substantial evidence that such rape-related sexual dysfunction exists.

Although not derived from social learning systems *per se*, it is reasonable to predict that rape would have a negative effect on self-esteem. Veronen (1978) found that victims' self-concepts were the most negative after their rape experiences. Veronen and Kilpatrick (Note 5) found that victims had lower self-esteem than nonvictims for at least a year after their rape.

EMPIRICAL SUPPORT FOR CRISIS VERSUS SOCIAL LEARNING THEORIES

Crisis theory receives partial support from empirical data. As predicted by both crisis and social learning theory, recent rape victims experienced considerable subjective distress, including feelings of anxiety, depression, poor self-esteem, helplessness, and loss of control. Moreover, victims improved substantially during the 1 month to 3 months postrape period. However, crisis theory predicts that the crisis state should be resolved 6 to 8 weeks after the precipitating event. While greatly improved, most victims at 3 months, 6 months, and 1 year postrape were not symptom free. A core of fear and anxiety responses persists up to 1 year postrape. Thus it would be difficult to argue that the rape-induced crisis had been resolved in light of victims' continuing distress. Data on rape effects appear to support Lewis et al. (1979), who contend that the crisis state is longer than 6 to 8 weeks. Additional research on the nature and duration of crisis states is clearly needed. It seems quite clear that rape produces both short- and long-term effects and that the short-term effects are more pronounced and intense.

TREATMENT OF RAPE-RELATED PROBLEMS

Overview

Our clinical and research experience leads us to think that there are substantial differences between recent and long-term victims. Since subjective distress diminishes considerably by 3 months after the rape, it is useful to define recent victims as those less than 3 months postrape. Recent and long-term victims differ in the types of problems they experience, their ability to participate in systematic treatment, and in types of treatment approaches most likely to be effective. Recent victims encountered immediately after the rape (e.g., 1 to 2 days postrape) probably differ considerably from recent victims whose rape was more distant. Because of the focus of this book, we will deal with approaches for treating recent victims. Information on treatment of long-term victims is provided elsewhere (Kilpatrick et al., 1982; Veronen & Kilpatrick, 1983). Crisis intervention approaches for treating recent victims will be briefly reviewed. A new behavioral treatment for recent victims, the Brief Behavioral Intervention Procedure (BBIP), will be described with respect to its commonalities to crisis intervention as well as its differences.

Victims' Needs

Good treatment is usually preceded by a careful assessment of the needs and problems of the clients to be served. While there has been no formal needs assessment conducted with victims, there is reasonable agreement about the most pressing needs and problems. Burgess and Holmstrom (1974a) used the term "crisis requests" to describe victim needs and identified the following requests for the immediate victim: (a) I need a police officer, (b) I need a physician, (c) I need someone to talk to, (d) I need control, and (e) I'm uncertain that I want anything. We partially agree with Burgess and Holmstrom's conclusions but see many victims whose greatest concern is whether or not to report the crime to police. These victims experience little need to see a police officer. Additionally, victims are quite concerned about the procedures they are undergoing and would like explanations about them (Burgess & Holmstrom, 1974a; Kilpatrick, Best, & Veronen, 1978). Victims are extremely concerned about what people will think of them after being raped (e.g., will people blame me?). Deciding whom of their friends, family, and colleagues to tell about the assault and how to tell them is an important concern for most victims.

Intervention with Immediate Victims

There is general agreement that early intervention with victims is useful and about what its focus should be. Any intervention program should provide a victim with information about the procedures she is to undergo as well as the rationale for such procedures. The victim should also have the opportunity to talk with a sympathetic individual knowledgeable about rape who can help her explore options and provide emotional support and acceptance. In many places, a volunteer rape crisis counselor/advocate provides this service. Counselor advocates are on call, explain procedures to victims, help victims formulate options, and provide emotional support. In many cases, counselor advocates also provide some follow-up counseling and attend court hearings with victims (Best & Kilpatrick, 1977). While the efficacy of this paraprofessional intervention approach has not yet been demonstrated, there is ample anecdotal data from victims and counselors/advocates alike to suggest that the process is viewed as helpful by both groups. The primary way in which our early intervention program differs from other crisis intervention approaches is that we teach volunteer counselors/advocates our social learning formulations of rape-induced problems, and how to use these formulations to explain and predict the victim's reactions.

Crisis Intervention with Recent Victims

Burgess and Holmstrom (1974a) describe the following general principles of crisis intervention with recent victims: (a) it is short-term and issues-oriented, (b) the counselor responds to the crisis request of the victims, (c) the counselor deals primarily with rape-related problems and not with other problems, and (d) the counselor takes an active role in initiating follow-up contacts. Burgess and Holmstrom provide a considerable amount of rich clinical data and counseling suggestions but have never really described the actual content or amount of treatment they provided to their victims.

A Brief Behavioral Intervention Procedure for Recent Victims

Our assessment research indicated that fear and anxiety are serious problems for recent and long-term victims, suggesting the need for some intervention. However, the extreme distress and behavioral disruption which characterize the first 2 or 3 months post-rape make it difficult to conduct any sort of treatment which requires sustained participation by the victim (Kilpatrick et al., 1982).

In response to this dilemma, we developed a 4 to 6 hour treatment package for recent victims called the Brief Behavioral Intervention Procedure (BBIP), which combines elements of feminist rape crisis counseling and behavioral treatment procedures. BBIP is envisioned as a prophylactic treatment which may short-circuit the development of phobias and other rape-related problems. It is based on the following assumptions: (a) the victim's rape experience must be validated rather than questioned, (b) victims hold myths or false beliefs about rape which make them feel responsible for their attack, (c) victims lack information about the normal reactions to a rape experience, and (d) victims lack skills for coping with rape-related problems. The overriding assumption is that providing victims with information and with coping skills will assist them in dealing with rape-induced problems.

BBIP is highly structured and designed such that it can be used by paraprofessionals. It has four components, the contents of which will be described subsequently.

We are currently evaluating the efficacy of BBIP in a study which randomly assigns recent victims and matched nonvictims to one of three treatment conditions: (a) repeated assessment, (b) delayed assessment, or (c) BBIP. All participants undergo comprehensive assessment at 6-21 days and 3 months postrape. Participants in the delayed assessment condition receive no additional contact, while those in the repeated assessment condition are assessed at 1 and 2 months postrape. Those in the BBIP condition participate in BBIP after their initial assessment. BBIP is conducted by one of four peer counselors, all of whom are women experienced in working with rape victims and trained to use the BBIP procedures.

The first component of BBIP is an induced affect interview. The victim is instructed to relax via deep muscle and deep breathing relaxation techniques. After achieving a moderate state of relaxation, the victim is queried about the rape incident. On the basis of the victim's responses, the counselor reconstructs a word scene of: (a) the situation which immediately preceded the rape, (b) the first moment the victim felt she was in danger, (c) the rape itself, and (d) the situation immediately following the rape. At each of these four sequences, the victim is instructed to feel whatever she was feeling at the time, to expand upon that feeling, and let her body experience that feeling in whatever part she felt it at the time.

This interview procedure frequently results in a release of emotions; the victim frequently cries, breathing rate increases, and muscle tension may be noted. This procedure appears to benefit the victim by permitting an emotional release and enabling her to clarify feelings experienced during the assault. The victim is capable of recalling details of the assault and feelings which she had previously blocked out or forgotten. In this procedure, the victim's feelings are specifically focused upon by the counselor. This is very different from the questioning conducted by the police who are only interested in the facts of the incident.

The second part of the BBIP consists of the presentation of the development of fear and anxiety from a learning or classical conditioning model. Reactions of the victim are explained as expected, predictable, and understandable given that rape is a life-threatening event and that situations, people, and events similar to the rape situation will evoke similar feelings. Additionally, the victim is taught that fear, anxiety, or other feelings occur in stages and degrees and that she need not be overwhelmed or incapacitated by the feelings, and that her feelings may be expressed in three channels: (a) physically, through stomach upset, muscular tension, or increased vigilance and agitation, (b) behaviorally, through action or movement away from the feared object, or (c) cognitively, through unpleasant thoughts, images, or flashbacks.

During the third portion of the BBIP, the counselor and victim examine the ways in which the victim is made to feel responsible or guilty for having been raped. This is an in-depth examination of the victim-blame myth and involves scrutinizing the ways in which women are: (a) taught to feel responsible for rape, (b) portrayed as responsible in the media (e.g., Scarlett O'Hara) or in fables (e.g., Little Red Riding Hood), and (c) conditioned to feel responsible by bearing the biological burden of pregnancy as a result of intercourse.

The implications of self-blame or feelings of responsibility for the victim are also examined. For example, if a woman feels responsible, she may limit or restrict her life to insure that a similar situation will not arise. To diminish the victim's feelings of guilt and responsibility, the counselor encourages the victim to recognize some of the societal forces that are responsible for the rape, such as men's socialization to aggressively press for sex and media representations of women enjoying forced sex.

The last section of the BBIP involves teaching coping skills, strategies, and reentry procedures in order to deal with feelings and behavioral changes which may have occurred since the assault. Victims are urged to become more assertive by taking charge of the activities related to the assault such as calling police, deciding whom they will tell, and taking more control over other life situations. Victims are also taught such specific coping skills as deep breathing, muscle relaxation, and thought stoppage, and they are given suggestions of ways in which they can initiate or resume activities they have avoided because of fear.

Since the study of BBIP's efficacy is still in progress, outcome data are not available. However, counselors like to use BBIP with victims, and victims appear to like BBIP as well. BBIP has the additional advantage of being highly structured and designed to be relatively easily learned by a variety of treatment providers. We plan to prepare detailed instructions regarding the use of BBIP as a treatment.

SUMMARY AND CONCLUSIONS

In conclusion, we will address the issue of BBIP's similarities with and differences from crisis intervention. Using Auerbach and Kilmann's (1977) criteria, BBIP would qualify as crisis intervention since it: (a) focuses on immediate problems, (b) consists of a minimal number of brief contacts, (c) has a high level of therapist activity, (d) encourages the client to identify coping strategies and to problem solve, and (e) attempts to reduce dependency on the therapist.

BBIP differs from crisis intervention procedures used with rape victims in that it: (a) is considerably more structured, (b) has well-developed theoretical underpinnings, (c) teaches specific coping strategies, and (d) is being systematically evaluated.

In this chapter, we have presented an overview of crisis theory and intervention with a critical examination of the use of this approach with rape victims. We have presented empirical data on the victim's reactions to rape. We have demonstrated support for a social learning theory for the prediction of victims' reactions. Finally, we have outlined a brief treatment, BBIP, which utilizes techniques and concepts from behavioral treatments and feminist counseling, and we have discussed the similarities and differences between crisis counseling and BBIP. It is our conclusion that crisis theory represents an inadequate conceptualization of rape victims' reactions and that crisis intervention is an incomplete treatment strategy.

REFERENCE NOTES

1.   Goodchilds, J. C. *Non-stranger rape: The role of sexual socialization.* National Center for the Prevention and Control of Rape, NIMH, Grant No. R01 MH30655, 9/29/77-3/31/80.

2. Koss, M. P. *Hidden rape on a university campus*. National Center for the Prevention and Control of Rape, NIMH, Grant No. R01 MH31618, 9/25/78-8/31/80.
3. Selby, J. W., III. *Perception of rape: Influences on causal attributions*. National Center for the Prevention and Control of Rape, NIMH, Grant No. R01 MH30702, 8/15/79-7/30/80.
4. Burt, M. R. *Attitudes supportive of rape in American culture*. Testimony submitted to the U.S. House Committee on Science and Technology, January 3, 1978.
5. Veronen, L. J., & Kilpatrick, D. G. The response to rape: The impact of rape on self-esteem. Paper presented at the 26th Annual Convention of the Southwestern Psychological Association, Oklahoma City, Okla., April 11, 1980.
6. Resick, P. A., Kilpatrick, D. G., & Veronen, L. J. Burgess and Holmstrom's rape trauma syndrome: A methodological critique. Unpublished manuscript, Medical University of South Carolina, 1979.
7. Calhoun, K. S., Atkeson, B. M., & Resick, P. A. Incidence and patterns of depression in rape victims. Paper presented at the 13th Annual Convention of the Association for Advancement of Behavior Therapy, San Francisco, December 15, 1979.
8. Becker, J. V. *Sexual dysfunctions in rape victims*. National Center for the Prevention and Control of Rape, NIMH, Grant No. R01 MH32982, 9/25/79-8/31/82.

REFERENCES

Auerbach, S.M., & Kilmann, P.R. Crisis intervention: A review of outcome research. *Psychological Bulletin*, 1977, *84*, 1189–1217.

Bard, M., & Sangrey, D. *The crime victim's book*. New York: Basic Books, 1979.

Beck, A. T. *Cognitive therapy and the emotional disorders*. New York: International University Press, 1976.

Best, C. L., & Kilpatrick, D. G. Psychological profiles of rape crisis counselors. *Psychological Reports*, 1977, *40*, 1127-1134.

Bloom, B. Definitional aspects of the crisis concept. *Journal of Consulting Psychology*, 1963, *27*, 498-502.

Brownmiller, S. *Against our will*. New York: Simon & Schuster, 1975.

Burgess, A. W., & Homstrom, L. L. *Rape: Victims of crisis*. Bowie, Md.: Robert J. Brady Co., 1974a.

Burgess, A. W., & Holmstrom, L. L. Rape trauma syndrome. *American Journal of Psychiatry*, 1974b, *131*, 981-986.

Burgess, A. W., & Holmstrom, L. L. *Rape: Crisis and recovery*. Bowie, Md.: Robert J. Brady Co., 1979.

Butcher, J. N., & Maudal, G. R. Crisis intervention. In I. Weiner (Ed.), *Clinical methods in psychology*. New York: Wiley, 1976.

Caplan, G. *An approach to community mental health*. New York: Basic Books, 1961.

Caplan, G. *Principles of preventive psychiatry*. New York: Basic Books, 1964.

Deutsch, H. *The psychology of women: A psychoanalytic interpretation by Helene Deutsch*. New York: Grune & Stratton, 1944.

Factor, M. A woman's psychological reaction to attempted rape. *Psychoanalytic Quarterly*, 1954, *23*, 243-244.

Feldman-Summers, S., Gordon, P. E., & Meagher, J. R. The impact of rape on sexual satisfaction. *Journal of Abnormal Psychology*, 1979, *88*(1), 101-105.

Frank, E., Turner, S. M., & Duffy, B. Depressive symptoms in rape victims. *Journal of Affective Disorders*, 1979, *1*, 269-297.

Kilpatrick, D. G., Best, C. L., & Veronen, L. J. The adolescent rape victim: Psychological responses to sexual assault and treatment approaches. In A. K. Kreutner & D. R. Hollingsworth (Eds.), *Adolescent obstetrics and gynecology1. Chicago: Year Book Medical Publishers,* 1978.

Kilpatrick, D. G., Resick, P. A., & Veronen, L. J. Longitudinal effects of a rape experience. *Journal of Social Issues*, 1981, *37*(4), 105-122.

Kilpatrick, D. G., Veronen, L. J., & Resick, P. A. Responses to rape: Behavioral perspectives and treatment approaches. *Scandinavian Journal of Behavior Therapy*, 1977, *6*, 85.

Kilpatrick, D. G., Veronen, L. J., & Resick, P. A. The aftermath of rape: Recent empirical findings. *American Journal of Orthopsychiatry*, 1979a, *49*(4), 658-669.

Kilpatrick, D. G., Veronen, L. J., & Resick, P. A. Assessment of the aftermath of rape: Changing patterns of fear. *Journal of Behavioral Assessment*, 1979b, *1*(2), 133-148.

Kilpatrick, D. G., Veronen, L. J., & Resick, P. A. Psychological sequelae to rape: Implications for treatment. In D. M. Doleys, R. L. Meredith, & A. R. Ciminero (Eds.), *Behavioral medicine: Assessment and treatment strategies*. New York, Plenum, 1982.

Korchin, S. *Modern clinical psychology: Principles of intervention in the clinic and community*. New York: Basic Books, 1976.

Lewinsohn, P. M. Clinical and theoretical aspects of depression. In K. S. Calhoun, H. E. Adams, & K. M. Mitchell (Eds.), *Innovative treatment methods in psychopathology*. New York: Wiley, 1974.

Lewis, M. S., Gottesman, D., & Gutstein, S. The course and duration of crisis. *Journal of Consulting and Clinical Psychology*, 1979, *47*(1), 128-134.

Schulberg, H., & Sheldon, A. The probability of crisis and strategies for preventive intervention. *Archives of General Psychiatry*, 1968, *18*, 553-558.

Seligman, M. E. P. *Helplessness: On depression, development, and death*. San Francisco: Freeman, 1975.

Sutherland, S., & Scherl, D. Patterns of response among victims of rape. *American Journal of Orthopsychiatry*, 1970, *40*, 503-511.

Taplin, J. Crisis theory: Critique and reformulation. *Community Mental Health Journal*, 1971, *7*, 13-23.

Veronen, L. J. Fear response of rape victims. (Doctoral dissertation, North Texas State University, 1977). *Dissertation Abstracts International*, 1978, *38*(7). (University Microfilms No. TSZ 77-29, 577).

Veronen, L. J., & Kilpatrick, D. G. Self-reported fears of rape victims: A preliminary investigation. *Behavior Modification*, 1980, *4*(3), 383-396.

Veronen, L.J., & Kilpatrick, D.G. Stress management for rape victims. In D. Meichenbaum & M. Jaremko (Eds.), *Stress reduction and prevention*. New York: Plenum, 1983.

Veronen, L.J., & Kilpatrick, D.G. Rape: A precursor of change. In E.J. Callahan & K. McCluskey (Eds.), *Life span developmental psychology: Non-normative life events*. New York: Academic Press, in press.

Veronen, L. J., Kilpatrick, D. G., & Resick, P. A. Treatment of fear and anxiety in rape victims: Implications for the criminal justice system. In W. H. Parsonage (Ed.), *Perspectives on victimology*. Beverly Hills, Calif.: Sage, 1979.

Section III

CRISIS INTERVENTION RESEARCH

In the final chapter, Stephen Auerbach provides a critical analysis of the research strategies that have been employed in the study of crisis intervention. He classifies the research using four broad categories: (a) studies designed to test theoretically-based assumptions, (b) studies which evaluate programs that primarily use paraprofessionals as service providers and have a strong community emphasis, (c) studies which evaluate generic crisis intervention programs, and (d) studies of crisis-oriented psychotherapy. His chapter includes an acknowledgement of the paucity of theory-relevant research, with specific suggestions for theory-validational studies, and he discusses the relative advantages and disadvantages of various research strategies designed to evaluate the *effectiveness* of crisis intervention.

Chapter 10

CRISIS INTERVENTION RESEARCH
Methodological Considerations and Some Recent Findings

Stephen M. Auerbach

The two Chinese characters which form the word "crisis" represent "danger" and "opportunity." These two words subsume the major elements of the concept as it is used in literature, the behavioral sciences, as well as in everyday language: a situation which is perceived as stressful and induces emotional disequilibrium, and which impels one toward decision-making, choice, and therefore opportunity to change. Crisis intervention refers to programs or techniques designed to alleviate or minimize the stressful elements of experiencing a crisis and/or to capitalize on those aspects of the experience in which there is potential for growth and constructive change. From the most conservative standpoint, it has been said that a principal goal of crisis intervention is the restoration of precrisis level of functioning (e.g., Bloom, 1980). It will be seen, however, that the stated and measured goals of actual crisis intervention programs are many and varied and depend on the nature of the crisis-inducing stressor and its temporal relation to the individual experiencing it, the setting in which the intervention program is undertaken, and the particular interests and goals of the researcher.

The purpose of this chapter is to present a critical analysis of the research strategies that have been employed in the study of crisis intervention. It will be shown that there is no single well-accepted research paradigm and that one must adapt one's research design to the particular requirements of the situation being studied. In my opinion it is useful to classify crisis intervention research into four broad categories: (a) studies designed to test theoretically-based assumptions regarding the nature of the crisis construct and the effects of crisis intervention, (b) studies that evaluate the effects of programs that primarily use paraprofessionals as service providers and have a strong community emphasis (e.g., telephone hot lines), (c) studies that evaluate programs designed to mitigate the deleterious effects of exposure to a specific aversive event (e.g., sexual assault, natural disaster, divorce), and (d) studies of crisis-oriented psychotherapy primarily involving professionals doing face-to-face therapy.

THEORY-BASED RESEARCH

"Crisis theory" is often referred to as if there existed an established conceptual model which has been validated to the satisfaction of the most stringent requirements. Many writers and researchers take advantage of this assumption and blandly state that the intervention techniques they used in a given setting were based on the "established tenets of crisis theory," in lieu of describing specific procedures. The most widely cited and influential model is Caplan's (1964) conceptualization of crisis as a state of psychological disequilibrium brought about by a loss of "basic supplies" and subsequent breakdown in the hypothetical homeostatic problem-solving mechanism. As with most psychodynamically-based theories, it is difficult to reduce to practicably testable hypotheses, and thus has been widely accepted as a self-evident truth without undergoing rigorous evaluation.

Two "basic assumptions," in particular, have come to be associated with the Caplanian model and have received widespread uncritical acceptance. First, a primary assumption is that crisis reactions are inherently self-limiting and are resolved either adaptively or maladaptively within 4 to 6 weeks (Bloom, 1977) (some writers cite 8 weeks as the critical duration). While it is self-evident that reactions to many stressful life events are transient, the uncritical acceptance of a specific time period as applicable for all crisis events for all individuals seems capricious. Few investigators have critically evaluated the validity of this assumption or its applicability to a variety of crisis-inducing events (Lewis, Gottesman, & Gutstein, 1979 is a recent exception). The second assumption involves the supposition that individuals in crisis are in a heightened state of suggestibility and are highly motivated, and that for treatment to be optimally effective it must take place immediately. The question of the optimal point at which to intervene is a crucial one, but it is likely to differ depending on the crisis event (e.g., prior to surgery, after a sexual assault, or exposure to a natural disaster) and the particular individual. Although meaningful research is lacking in this area, it seems unlikely that crisis states generated in different contexts have uniform effects across individuals.

Studies focused solely on theoretical questions relating to crisis have been few and far between. Much of the research that is available is narrowly conceived and contributes little to our understanding of the crisis construct. An example is Smith's (1970) finding that patients serviced at an emergency room because of "acute life crises" became more internal on Rotter's Locus of Control Scale after a 6-week period than a noncrisis group beginning long-term therapy. On the other hand, in a broadly conceived study, Bloom (1963) obtained important construct validational data relating to the crisis concept. He addressed the question of what characteristics of life events are most influential in causing them to be classified as crises. Reasoning that the crucial elements in the identification of the crisis state appear to be a stressful precipitating event of which the individual is aware and rapid cognitive and affective disruption which lasts at least several days, he presented brief case histories to expert judges in which each of these elements was manipulated. He found that, in practice, a crisis is defined primarily in terms of knowledge of a precipitating stressful event and problem resolution requiring more than a week.

A vexing question for researchers is how to measure the crisis response or reliably establish the presence of a state of crisis. Most researchers assume a state of crisis based on the presence of or temporal proximity to a certain "stressful" event (e.g., death of loved one, impending surgery) without obtaining any independent measure of emotional reaction. In some cases, "state" measures of emotional status such as the State-Trait Anxiety Inventory are used especially in situations where there is an available measurement period, such as prior to a surgical operation (Auerbach, 1973; Lewis et al., 1979). Much recent work has also been done on the development of "stressful life event scales" such as Holmes and Rahe's (1967) Social Readjustment Rating Scale. However, these scales have been used to evaluate post hoc the degree to which individuals have been exposed to a range of crisis events rather than as response measures. Recent findings suggest that it is not simple exposure to stressors that determine the degree to which they induce social disruption; extremely important in determining whether a given event reaches crisis proportions is the context in which it occurs and the degree of social support an individual perceives he or she has (e.g., Dohrenwend & Martin, 1979).

In the only attempt I am aware of to develop a measure of response to crisis per se, Halpern (1973) adapted 60 statements from the Minnesota Multiphasic Personality Inventory and the Community Adaptation Schedule which tapped what he designated as the ten aspects of crisis reactions (feelings of tiredness and exhaustion, helplessness, inadequacy, confusion, anxiety, physical symptoms, and disorganization of work functioning, family and social relationships, and social activities). Subjects were asked to respond in terms of "the way things are now compared with how they have been in the past." He found that groups of individuals involved in situations associated with crisis (divorce, bereavement, students applying for aid at a mental health center, newly admited patients to a public mental health institution) obtained higher scores than comparable groups not under stress. A lack of significant differences among the crisis groups was interpreted as indicating a degree of "communality in the behavior of individuals in a wide variety of situations which have all been labeled crisis situations." Lewis et al. (1979) additionaly have demonstrated that patients undergoing surgery for cancer obtain higher scores on this scale than those undergoing surgery for less serious illnesses. Drawbacks of the scale include its excessive length given that it is designed to measure a transitory situational response (although an apparently briefer revised from has been developed according to Lewis et al., 1979) and a lack of discriminant validity data.

Community-based Suicide Prevention/Hot Line Programs

Historically, crisis intervention has been closely identified with suicide prevention. The growth of suicide prevention programs in the United States can be traced back to 1906 and the National Save-A-Life League in New York City (McGee, 1974), but the most important element was the development in 1958 and continued federal support given to the Los Angeles Suicide Prevention Center (LASPC). The LASPC developed the methodology for telephone crisis intervention work and spelled out the technical functions of the paraprofessional worker. Research and evaluation in this area has become increasingly complex. The great majority of programs operate with nonprofessionals as their primary staff resource and these service providers differ in how, the degree to which, and the effectiveness with which they are trained. Most agencies are no longer geared toward suicide prevention. Some focus on specialized target populations such as the elderly, gays, or students. In terms of service provision, some focus on referral, others on dispensing information, and others on direct clinical services for a wide range of problems. Most agencies provide telephone counseling while others provide face-to-face services.

With the continuing proliferation of programs, perhaps the first evaluation question to be addressed is that of need. Some localities are being inundated with hot lines and similar service agencies. Before instituting new programs, organizers should ascertain whether additional services are meaningful given the current range of services available in the community. This would involve gathering relevant census data, surveying residents of the community to be served, surveying existing agencies providing similar services, and surveying knowledgeable community residents. Such needs assessment procedures should provide information not only on simply what is already available, but also on whether the service should be organized toward meeting the needs of particular groups or problem areas that appear to be underserved, and on the potential for establishing referral and continuity of care relationships with existing agencies.

For existing services, the particular evaluation procedures to be undertaken are largely determined by the nature of the questions one has about the functioning of an agency. At one level are questions regarding number of clients serviced, the nature of their problems, the type of service they received, and duration of treatment, etc.—questions that may be answered with simple descriptive data. At a second level are questions relating to the internal functioning of a program, which often involve interrelating several pieces of data. Questions in this category would include: What types of individuals make the best volunteers? Is our training effective? What components of training are most effective? The most sophisticated form of evaluation involves determining outcome—ascertaining whether a program is effective in achieving its goals. Outcome in regard to community-based crisis intervention programs has been defined in terms both of client change and counselor change variables as well as measures of community impact. Recent research in selected areas is reviewed below.

Counselor Characteristics

Reflecting the continuing concern with selecting from among applicants those individuals likely to be successful counselors, a number of recent studies have obtained demographic data and measured various personality traits of volunteers. Some studies have been purely descriptive and of no apparent practical utility. For example, Chartoff (1976) found a number of interests, values, and personality characteristics that discriminated volunteers from nonvolunteers; she also found that female volunteers had stronger social values and weaker economic values than both nonvolunteers and personnel and guidance workers, and stronger social and religious values and weaker theoretical values than social workers. Irey (1976) compared crisis workers with other professionals (e.g., physicians, psychologists) and came up with a single discriminant function which significantly differentiated among the groups. Russem (1977) demonstrated significant differences between hot line counselors, hot line trainees, hospital volunteers, and board of directors members on "purpose of life" and "intrafamily relationships."

Four studies attempted to relate counselor characteristics to some measure of counselor functioning. Schoenfeld and Neal (1976) found that "authoritarian" volunteers use fewer words and give more referrals than "altruistic" volunteers. In another study, Schoenfeld, Preston, and Adams (1976) presented preliminary findings on Minnesota Multiphasic Personality Inventory (MMPI) variables and demographic data which differentiated between active versus inactive, accepted versus rejected, and highest rated versus lowest rated volunteers. Evans (1976), using the MMPI, was able to differentiate between conscientious volunteers (those who maintained adequate service for a 3 month posttraining period) and nonconscientious ones. Using a stepwise discriminant analysis, scales L, Hs, Pt, and Hs (K corrected) and the Hot Line Perseverance Scale (20 items empirically selected from the MMPI) were found to discriminate maximally (90% correct classifications of the conscientious group and 96% of the nonconscientious group). In a similar study, Evans (1977) was able to efficiently distinguish between effective crisis interviewers (those who gave 40% or more "good" responses as classified by the Therapist Error Checklist) and ineffective interviewers using MMPI scales L, F, D, Hy, Pd, Pa, Pt, Sc, Ma, and Pd (Sc and Ma with K corrected). Pending cross-validation and possible application of his procedures to other counselor criterion variables, Evans' work has provided a legitimate empirical basis for use of the MMPI as a selection tool with volunteers.

Effects of Training

Three recent studies evaluated the effects of volunteer training programs. In two (Lister, 1976; Seymour, 1976), volunteers responded to the Crisis Intervention Discrimination Index (which is apparently a prepared crisis case presented on audio- or videotape) and in both studies trained volunteers were superior to an untrained control group on the process variables of "discrimination of core conditions" and "communication of empathy." In a third study, Margolis, Edwards, Shrier, and Cramer (1975) found a significant differential pre-posttraining increase in "perceived knowledge" for a group of trained volunteers versus an untrained control group. These studies indicate that training programs effectively produce appropriate cognitive changes and desired improvements in therapy process skills among trainees. They do not, however, deal with the more refined questions of differential effectiveness of alternative training procedures, of isolating essential training components, nor of the relationship between training and volunteer effectiveness defined in terms of client change measures.

Outcome: Suicide Rate

Given the initial thrust of the crisis intervention movement toward suicide prevention, several investigators have evaluated the impact of the presence of suicide prevention centers on the suicide rate in the community being served. In an earlier review (Auerbach & Kilmann, 1977) it was noted that in two studies (Lester, 1974; Weiner, 1969) which examined suicide rates in cities prior to and subsequent to the institution of suicide prevention services, results suggested that the existence of suicide prevention centers had no effect on suicide rate. However, these results were deemed questionable because of doubts regarding the comparability of experimental to control towns and the heterogeneity and unknown nature of services offered in experimental towns. Bagley's (1968) study was a significant improvement in both of these areas in that: (a) he evaluated the effects of a comparatively homogeneous treatment program (the Samaritan 24-hour telephone crisis service with branches located in the United Kingdom and Eire), and (b) he went to great lengths to match towns receiving Samaritan services on a number of "ecological" variables with control towns not receiving services. Bagley reported a 5.8% decline in suicide rate in towns receiving Samaritan services whereas the average rate in control towns increased 19.8% over the same period of time.

Two recent studies, however, cast doubt on Bagley's (1968) findings and on his approach as a viable research format. Jennings, Barraclough, and Moss (1978) further examined suicide rate data in regard to the Samaritans and noted that although the growth of the organization has coincided with suicide decline and that the Samaritans do attract people who commit suicide, the suicide rate has not continued to decline as steeply since 1970 despite the continued growth in the number of Samaritan branches and the large increase in number of clients. This finding is in accord with Auerbach and Kilmann's (1977) earlier conclusion that: "Despite careful matching of experimental and control towns on economic, social, and demographic characteristics, reduction in suicide rate could as readily have been a function of those social changes in the community that promoted development of a Samaritan service as of the impact of the service itself" (p. 1192). Initially, when the Samaritans were new it is likely that only the most socially progressive towns developed branches, but as the organization became well established branches were established routinely. Jennings et al. (1978), using more recent suicide rate data than Bagley and more precisely matching experimental and control towns, found no significant pre-post differences in percentage change in suicide rate for the two sets of towns using any of the four matching methods. Bridge, Potkin, Zung, and Soldo (1977), using statistical controls for differences in demographic composition of counties, similarly found that the presence of suicide prevention centers had a minimal effect on the suicide rate in North Carolina in 1970.

These findings do not indicate that suicide prevention centers are useless. Jennings et al. (1978) note: "The value of their contributions in providing contact and comfort and relieving distress is not in question" (p. 413). While this statement, to be considered valid, requires supporting data on actual Samaritan clients, it reflects the good will generated by the organization and the important social function it serves. However, it has become clear that it is not feasible to attempt to demonstrate a program's effectiveness by showing that it has produced behavior change in an entire community. Too many other social changes are likely to be covarying with the establishment of the program. As Auerbach and Kilmann (1977) noted, this is also a problem with nonsuicide-related outcome measures: "Variables such as drug use, divorce rate, and hospitalization may be affected by uncontrollable factors such as drug supply, ease of obtaining a divorce based on relaxed laws or easing of social sanctions, and changing criteria for hospital admission, respectively. A more viable general procedure is to demonstrate positive changes in individuals who have actually utilized the program..." (p. 1198).

Outcome research with nonsuicide-related measures, reviewed below, has in fact largely focused on measuring changes in both clients and counselors who have actually been involved in programs.

Outcome: Nonsuicide-related Measures

Until recently, the outcome research emphasis in this area has been on defining outcome in terms of crisis worker performance. Operationally, this has meant evaluating technical effectiveness (TE) using the Fowler Technical Effectiveness Scale (Fowler & McGee, 1973) and clinical effectiveness (CE) using scales measuring the "facilitative conditions" of empathy, warmth, and genuineness. Research, primarily by McGee and his students (Note 1), has indicated that both TE and CE may be measured reliably, but criterion-related validity data have been sparse. Auerbach and Kilmann (1977) concluded that excess emphasis was being placed on defining outcome in terms of worker process variables, since insufficient data relating worker CE and TE to client change measures were available and also given that the goal of many crisis programs is transfer or referral as opposed to direct treatment.

In two recent dissertations (Delfin, 1978; Echterling, 1977), crisis worker behavior was coded and an attempt was made to establish a relationship between worker behavior and caller outcome as evaluated by the Crisis Call Outcome Form. In a third study, Blumenthal, Tulkin, and Slaikeu (1976) found that for clients who showed for a scheduled appointment (outcome measure), the referral is suggested sooner by the volunteer, the volunteer talks less during the prereferral period, and there is less silence throughout the call. Recent researchers have, however, by and large moved away from concern with helper performance variables and have employed measures more concretely related to the goals of a given program. For example, Friedman (1979) examined the effectiveness of a mobile crisis unit in reducing involuntary civil commitments for mental health reasons. Calsyn, Pribyl, and Sunukjiam (1977) argued that subsequent inpatient or outpatient treatment was a relevant outcome variable for their setting. Paul and Turner (1976) examined the effectiveness of a crisis service within the context of a behaviorally based employee motivation and management system designed to reward staff for on-task behaviors. In this setting, staff latency in responding to after hours emergency calls and frequency with which recommendations made by after hours emergency staff were followed were the two main outcome variables, and both changed in a positive direction when placed on a contingent basis.

Several investigators have focused on techniques to obtain direct outcome data from clients yet maintain client anonymity and minimal obtrusiveness. Speer (1971) used code numbers and tabulated the extent to which callers reused a hot line, assuming that those who reuse it do so because earlier experiences are satisfactory. Apsler and Hoople (1976) also obtained estimates of reuse, and Slem and Cotler (1973) surveyed those in the area serviced by a hot line and determined the degree to which the availability and purpose of the hot line was known. In a recent study, King (1977) distributed 3000 questionnaires to students on a college campus, and out of these 66 actual callers to a telephone counseling center were identified. Callers rated the effectiveness of the help received, the effectiveness of the counselor, and the impact of the contact on their life.

Some investigators have used simulated calls rather than actual clients (Apsler & Hodas, 1975; France, 1977; Morgan, 1977). In a most useful study, Apsler and Hodas (1975) evaluated whether the type of information requested by counselors is appropriate given the nature of the caller problem. A male and female caller telephoned the hot line with programmed calls asking for help with a dental problem. It was found that counselors did not request sufficient essential information from callers given the specific, concrete nature of the call, and that on only less than half of the calls were one or more correct referrals and no incorrect referrals given. Also, counselors gave fewer incorrect referrals to mid-week callers than weekend callers and more correct referrals to male versus female callers. The longer a call lasted the more correct referrals were given, and the more information counselors requested and provided the more favorably their manner was rated. Although the generality of these findings needs to be further explored, this is a significant study because it is one of very few that examines ''outcome'' in terms of the helper as an information provider and referral agent (two of the helper's major functions from a practical standpoint) as opposed to therapist.

In conclusion, there is no single method that constitutes the "best" or most appropriate way to measure outcome in this setting. The primary guideline is that outcome measures should be meaningfully and logically related to program goals. An agency that views itself as providing emergency emotional first aid and immediate symptom reduction should focus on producing short-term changes in client affect and on developing counselor clinical effectiveness. For programs emphasizing information and transfer and referral services, measures such as those employed by Apsler and Hodas (1975) and indicants such as clients' and referred agencies' satisfaction with referral are appropriate.

Perhaps the most serious impediment to conducting certain kinds of research with actual clients involves the question of protection of clients' rights and prior consent. Counselors may be told at the outset that occasionally they will get simulated calls or that their actual calls will be taped, and their consent may be requested at that time. However, obtaining prior consent for taping or obtaining any pretreatment data from clients who are under any degree of emotional distress (especially in the phone-in setting) does not appear to be feasible. Thus certain types of data collection procedures would appear to be limited in this setting, although the collection of follow-up data which could be elicited from the client at a noncrisis period should not be affected.

PROGRAMS ORIENTED AROUND SPECIFIC CRISIS EVENTS (GENERIC CRISIS INTERVENTION)

In attempting to categorize crisis intervention activities, Jacobson, Strickler, and Morley (1968) distinguished between individual and generic forms of crisis intervention. The individual form refers to short-term crisis-oriented psychotherapy, typically carried out by a professional, in which focus is on specific intrapsychic and interpersonal processes of the client as opposed to his or her immediate reaction to a specific stressor. This form of intervention will be discussed later. Generic crisis intervention, to be considered here, involves dealing with individuals who are reacting to specific crisis-inducing events (e.g., death of loved one, premature birth, divorce, natural disaster) for which there are believed to be known patterns of response and thus procedures designed to be effective for the target group as a whole. From both research and clinical perspectives, I believe it is meaningful to consider three types of generic interventions which are defined primarily on the basis of the temporal relationship of the individual to the crisis-inducing stimulus.

Type 1 generic intervention is analogous to the concept of primary prevention of disease as used in public health and as developed by Gerald Caplan (1964) in relation to the psychiatric disease model. Rather than deal with the prevention of disease (as do immunization or water flouridation procedures), such programs would deal with individuals who have not yet been exposed to a stressor, yet for whom the stressor is sufficiently aversive, a reasonably high probability event, and for which it is thus reasonable to institute procedures which will minimize its likelihood of occurring or of its causing damage if it does occur. A wide range of studies are subsumed here. For example, in the area of sexual assault, if one assumes that rape is fostered by attitudes in our culture which encourage or justify rape, then it is meaningful to implement programs designed to change attitudes which might foster the act itself, or which are obstacles to service delivery efforts. Similarly, education programs, geared toward potential victims and covering situations in which sexual attacks are likely to occur, would be hypothesized to lower rape incidence among those exposed to the program.

Evaluation of such programs, however, would be difficult if they were offered to broad samples of individuals from the community with the idea that they should result in a lowering of the overall sexual assault rate in the community. If this approach were taken the researcher would confront the same interpretative problems as those who attempted to influence community suicide rate through the presence of suicide prevention programs. A more meaningful way to design programs such as those described would be to target them toward specifically relevant groups (e.g., individuals with a history of sexual assault or those known to have unhealthy attitudes toward rape for the attitudes program; individuals who have been sexually assaulted or who reside in an area with a high incidence of sexual assault for the educational program), and evaluate the effectiveness of the program for the targeted group versus a matched control group not exposed to the program.

Type 2 generic intervention involves situations in which the crisis-inducing stressor has impacted the individual psychologically but not physically. The individual knows that he or she is about to be confronted with a stressful event (e.g., surgery, natural disaster, confinement in prison) but there is a period of waiting between knowledge of occurrence and actual impact. Thus there is often ample opportunity to intervene during the pre-impact period and institute programmed treatment packages. Assuming that one is assiduous in matching treatment and control groups, eliminating confounding due to multiple component treatment packages, and in selecting outcome measures which are meaningfully related to the goals of treatment, there are no major practical stumbling blocks in setting up and evaluating such programs. The area that has generated the greatest number of intervention studies of this type is impending surgery. That literature has recently been reviewed in detail (Auerbach, 1979; Auerbach & Kilmann, 1977).

Type 3 generic intervention involves situations in which the crisis-inducing event has impinged both psychologically and physically and the individual is recovering from the effects of exposure. Included here would be such diverse programs as: (a) Cromwell, Butterfield, Brayfield, and Curry's (1977) study exploring the effects of giving recovering heart attack patients different degrees of control over and participation in their own care during the postoperative period, (b) Lowman's (1979) study of a program utilizing nurses to deliver grief intervention to parents losing a baby due to Sudden Infant Death Syndrome, and (c) Kilpatrick and Veronen's (Note 2) study comparing systematic desensitization, stress innoculation, and individual peer counseling as treatment techniques with rape victims. Along with the experimental design considerations noted above in discussing type 2 research, evaluators of type 3 programs should be aware of any typical response sequences associated with recovery from exposure to the stressors they are studying. For example, the researcher evaluating the effects of an intervention program with rape victims should be aware of the acute-recoil-integration staging sequence said to be associated with response to rape (Thomas, 1977), and should design dependent measures and sequence measurement periods accordingly.

Crisis-Oriented Psychotherapy
(Individual Crisis Intervention)

What has come to be called crisis-oriented psychotherapy shares many of the features of conventional face-to-face psychotherapy. The main distinguishing characteristics appear to be that it is structured as brief and time-limited from the outset, emphasis is on the client's present problem, goals are limited to amelioration of the most disabling symptoms and return to previous level of functioning, and the therapist is active, direct, and reality-oriented in style (Butcher & Koss, 1978; Ewing, 1978).

Crisis-oriented psychotherapy is geared toward patients in acute distress whose overall premorbid adjustment has been satisfactory and whose current emotional dysphoria seems to be largely a function of response to a specific stressor as opposed to a continuing psychiatric disorder. The development and evaluation of crisis-oriented psychotherapy programs have many problems in common with psychotherapy research in general. Among the methodological problems noted by Butcher and Koss (1978) are the mobility and elusiveness of the population resulting in a high attrition rate which greatly inhibits obtaining follow-up data, and negative (deterioration) effects of therapy which seem to be related to the experience level of therapists. A third problem is the great heterogeneity of clients referred for crisis psychotherapy. As noted by Auerbach and Kilmann (1977), in psychiatric settings crisis patients are usually described as "acutely " disturbed or having symptoms requiring "emergency" treatment, but the nature of the stressor precipitating the acute reaction is not specified nor are patients differentiated on this basis. It is likely that many clients would not fit accepted criteria for crisis intervention, and in this regard Halpern's (1973) crisis response scale might be a useful tool.

In reviewing the outcome literature in this area, Auerbach and Kilmann (1977) concluded that the two main weaknesses were that most studies were not sufficiently controlled so that outcome differences could be reasonably attributed to treatment differences, and there was a general failure to specify operationally what crisis therapists were doing in therapy. These conclusions still stand.

Examination of treatment components in crisis-oriented therapy would appear to be a particularly fertile area for research because by definition the treatment period is time-limited and the subtle nuances of client-therapist interaction are therefore of paramount importance. Several good process measures of therapist behavior are available, including the TE and CE scales and a number of older classification systems (summarized by Kiesler, 1973). In addition, Kiesler and his colleagues (Perkins, Kiesler, Anchin, Chirico, Kyle, & Federman, 1979) have recently developed a promising measure (The Impact Message Inventory) for tying client emotional response to various elements of the therapeutic procedure.

CONCLUSION

In conclusion, it is apparent that no single crisis intervention research paradigm can be delineated and no overall judgment can be made regarding the effectiveness of crisis intervention procedures because of their great heterogeneity and wide applicability. Each of the four types of crisis intervention research strategies has its own distinctive character and particular methodological problems.

There is clearly a need for more theoretically oriented research if the crisis construct is ever to have an empirically based common core of meaning. Calsyn et al. (1977) and Parad and Parad (1968) have demonstrated that theory-based hypotheses can be readily evaluated within the context of an applied research program.

In two of the research areas, generic and individual crisis intervention, one often has the opportunity to design true experiments. The problem areas common to the two types of research in this regard are forming equivalent groups and avoiding confounding of treatment effects through use of multiple component packages. In individual crisis intervention, there is the added problem of establishing that clients can reasonably be considered to be "in crisis" and thus legitimate candidates for crisis therapy. In addition, there is the subject attrition problem. Because one often has a captive and motivated population to work with, generic programs are generally easier to implement and evaluate.

Studies of hot lines and similar programs using paraprofessionals usually involve program evaluations. The challenge for the researcher in this setting is to form goals of his or her agency, and to choose dependent measures that are logically related to these goals. After more than a decade of active research in this area, there are available a broad range of established measures to evaluate the effects of training, the process of counseling and adequacy of volunteer information and referral activities, client change and satisfaction with services, and to a limited extent overall community impact.

REFERENCE NOTES

1. McGee, R. K. (Ed.) *An evaluation of the volunteer in suicide prevention* (Final Project Report, Research Grant MH-16861, National Institute of Mental Health). Gainesville: University of Florida, Department of Clinical Psychology, Center for Crisis Intervention Research, May, 1974.
2. Kilpatrick, D., & Veronen, L. Treatment of fear and anxiety in victims of rape. (Research Grant R01 MH-29602), National Center for Prevention and Control of Rape—National Institute of Mental Health, 1977-1979.

REFERENCES

Apsler, R., & Hodas, M. B. Evaluating hot lines with stimulated calls. *Crisis Intervention*, 1975, *6*, 14-21.

Apsler, R., & Hoople, H. Evaluation of crisis intervention services with anonymous clients. *American Journal of Community Psychology*, 1976, *4*, 293-302.

Auerbach, S. M. Trait-state anxiety and adjustment to surgery. *Journal of Consulting and Clinical Psychology*, 1973, *40*, 264-271.

Auerbach, S. M. Preoperative preparation for surgery: A review of recent research and future prospects. In D. J. Osborne, M. M. Gruneberg, &

J. R. Eiser (Eds.), *Research in psychology and medicine*, Vol. II. London: Academic Press, 1979.

Auerbach, S. M., & Kilmann, P. R. Crisis intervention: A review of outcome research *Psychological Bulletin*, 1977, *84*, 1189-1217.

Bagley, C. The evaluation of a suicide prevention schema by an ecological method. *Social Science and Medicine*, 1968, *2*, 1-14.

Bloom, B. L. Definitional aspects of the crisis concept. *Journal of Consulting Psychology*, 1963, *27*, 498-502.

Bloom, B. L. *Community mental health: A general introduction*. Monterey, California: Brooks/Cole, 1977.

Bloom, B. L. Social and community interventions. *Annual Review of Psychology*, 1980, *31*, 111-142.

Blumenthal, D., Tulkin, S. R., & Slaikeu, K. A. Analysis of temporal variables in telephone calls to a suicide and crisis service: A comparison of clients who show for appointments and those who do not show. *Psychotherapy: Theory, Research, and Practice*, 1976, *13*. 177-182.

Bridge, T. P., Potkin, S. G., Zung, W. W. K., & Soldo, B. J. Suicide prevention centers: Ecological study of effectiveness. *Journal of Nervous and Mental Disease*, 1977, *164*, 18-24.

Butcher, J. N., & Koss, M. P. Research on brief and crisis-oriented therapies. In S. Garfield & A. Bergin (Eds.), *Handbook of psychotherapy and behavior change: An empirical analysis*. New York: Wiley, 1978.

Calsyn, R. J., Pribyl, J. R., & Sunukjian, J. Successful outcome in crisis intervention therapy. *American Journal of Community Psychology*, 1977, *5*, 111-119.

Caplan, G. *Principles of preventive psychiatry*. New York: Basic Books, 1964.

Chartoff, S. I. A comparison of interests, values, personality characteristics, and past experience with life crises of hot line volunteers, nonvolunteers, and selected professional groups. *Dissertation Abstracts International*, 1976, *37*, 3412A-3413A. (University Microfilms No. 76-27, 307).

Cromwell, R. L., Butterfield, E. C., Brayfield, F. M., & Curry, J. J. *Acute myocardial infarction: Reaction and recovery*. St. Louis: C. V. Mosby, 1977.

Delfin, P. E. A critical incidents analysis of telephone crisis intervention. *Dissertation Abstracts International*, 1978, *39*, 2492B. (University Microfilms No. 78-1435).

Dohrenwend, B. S., & Martin, J. Personal versus situational determination of anticipation and control of the occurrence of stressful life events. *American Journal of Community Psychology*, 1979, *7*, 453-468.

Echterling, L. G. Process and outcome of crisis intervention by telephone. *Dissertation Abstracts International*, 1977, *37*, 4136B. (University Microfilms No. 77-1798).

Evans, D. R. The use of the MMPI to predict conscientious hotline workers. *Journal of Clinical Psychology*, 1976, *32*, 684-686.

Evans, D. R. Use of the MMPI to predict effective hot line workers. *Journal of Clinical Psychology*, 1977, *33*, 1113-1114.

Ewing C. P. *Crisis intervention as psychotherapy*. New York: Oxford University Press, 1978.

Fowler, D. E., & McGee, R. K. Assessing the performance of telephone crisis workers: The development of a technical effectiveness scale. In D. Lester & G. Brockopp (Eds.), *Crisis intervention and counseling by telephone*. Springfield, Ill.: Charles C. Thomas, 1973.

France, K. Crisis service paraprofessionals: Expectations, evaluations, and training. *Crisis Intervention*, 1977, *8*, 2-18.

Friedman, J. Outcome evaluation of a mental health mobile crisis unit: Diversion from involuntary civil commitment. *Dissertation Abstracts International*, 1979, *40*, 2361B. (University Microfilms No. 79-5749).

Halpern, H. Crisis theory: A definitional study. *Community Mental Health Journal*, 1973, *9*, 342-349.

Holmes, T. H., & Rahe, R. H. The social readjustment rating scale. *Journal of Psychosomatic Research*, 1967, *11*, 213-218.

Irey, P. A. Personality dimensions of crisis interveners vs. academic psychologists, traditional clinicians, and paraprofessionals. *Dissertation Abstracts International*, 1976, *36*, 4161B. (University Microfilms No. 76-3318).

Jacobson, G. F., Strickler, M., & Morley, W. Generic and individual approaches to crisis intervention. *American Journal of Public Health*, 1968, *58*, 338-343.

Jennings, C., Barraclough, B. M., & Moss, J. R. Have the Samaritans lowered the suicide rate? A controlled study. *Psychological Medicine*, 1978, *8*, 413-422.

Kiesler, D. J. *The process of psychotherapy: Empirical foundations and systems of analysis*. Chicago: Aldine, 1973.

King, G. D. An evaluation of the effectiveness of a telephone counseling center. *American Journal of Community Psychology*, 1977, *5*, 75-83.

Lester, D. Effect of suicide prevention centers on suicide rates in the United States. *Public Health Reports*, 1974, *89*, 37-39.

Lewis, M. S., Gottesman, D., & Gutstein, S. The course and duration of crisis. *Journal of Consulting and Clinical Psychology*, 1979, *47*, 128-234.

Lister, T. L. A study of the effectiveness of the Vermillion hot line training program in increasing the skills of communicating empathy and discrimination. *Dissertation Abstracts International*, 1976, *36*, 4136B. (University Microfilms No. 76-2403).

Lowman, J. Grief intervention and sudden infant death syndrome. *American Journal of Community Psychology*, 1979, *7*, 665-677.

Margolis, C. G., Edwards, D. W., Shrier, L. P., & Cramer, M. Brief hotline training: An effort to examine impact on volunteers. *American Journal of Community Psychology*, 1975, *3*, 59-67.

McGee, R. K. *Crisis intervention in the community.* Baltimore: University Park Press, 1974.

Morgan, J. P. Effect of caller depth of self-exploration on high, medium, and low functioning telephone counselors. *Dissertation Abstracts International*, 1977, *37*, 5839B. (University Microfilms No. 77-9948).

Parad, L. G., & Parad, H. A study of crisis-oriented planned short-term treatment: Part II. *Social Casework*, 1968, *49*, 418-426.

Paul, T. W., & Turner, A. J. Evaluating the crisis service of a community mental health center. *American Journal of Community Psychology*, 1976, *4*, 303-308.

Perkins, M. J., Kiesler, D. J., Anchin, J. C., Chirico, B. M., Kyle, E. M., & Federman, E. The Impact Message Inventory: A new measure of relationship in counseling/psychotherapy and other dyads. *Journal of Counseling Psychology*, 1979, *26*, 363-367.

Russem, P. D. Differences in the meaning of life and quality of intrafamily relationships of four selected groups of volunteers. *Dissertation Abstracts International*, 1977, *37*, 3627B. (University Microfilms No. 76-30, 179).

Schoenfeld, C. S., & Neal, P. D. Altruism and authoritarianism and their relationship to number of referrals made by crisis-center volunteers. *Psychological Reports*, 1976, *39*, 705-706.

Schoenfeld, L. S., Preston, J., & Adams, R. L. Selection of volunteers for telephone crisis intervention centers. *Psychological Reports*, 1976, *39*, 725-726.

Seymour, P. J. Telephone crisis intervention: Empathy and conceptual level. *Dissertation Abstracts International*, 1976, *37*, 2528B. (University Microfilms No. 76-25, 633).

Slem, C. M., & Cotler, S. Crisis phone services: Evaluation of a hotline program. *American Journal of Community Psychology*, 1973, *1*, 219-227.

Smith, R. E. Changes in locus of control as a function of life crisis resolution. *Journal of Abnormal Psychology*, 1970, *79*, 328-332.

Speer, D. C. Rate of call re-use of a telephone crisis service. *Crisis Intervention*, 1971, *4*, 83-86.

Thomas, R. M. The crisis of rape and implications for counseling: A review of the literature. Part I. *Crisis Intervention*, 1977, *8*, 105-116.

Winter, I. The effectiveness of a suicide prevention program. *Mental Hygiene*, 1969, *53*, 357-373. ·

INDEX

213